ASPERGER'S SYNDROME

Tips & Strategies

For Parents/Carers, Teachers, Friends, Employers, and for those with Asperger's

Dan Jones

Connect with Dan Jones: www.ALT-Solutions.org

First Edition 2017

Published by Dan Jones

Copyright © Daniel Jones 2017

Daniel Jones asserts the moral right to be identified as the author of this work

All rights reserved. No part of this publication may be reproduced, stored in a retrieval system, or transmitted, in any form or by any means, electronic, mechanical, photocopying, recording, or otherwise, without the prior written permission of the publishers or author.

Front cover design: James, GoOnWrite.com
Front cover head: ID 4649675 © Yakobchuk | Dreamstime.com
Back cover playing card design: ID 23723800
© Christophe Boisson | Dreamstime.com

ISBN: 978-1546582960

Twitter: @AuthorDanJones

Table of Contents

CHAPTER ONE *Introduction* 1

CHAPTER TWO Parenting Children & Teens With Asperger's... 7

CHAPTER THREE *Teaching Those With Asperger's*...... 65

CHAPTER FOUR *Tips For Those With Asperger's* 85

CHAPTER FIVE Additional Tips For Adults With Asperger's... 117

CHAPTER SIX Interview Tips For Those With Asperger's... 121

CHAPTER SEVEN Being A Friend, Colleague, Or In A Relationship With Someone With Asperger's.................. 129

CHAPTER EIGHT Being An Employer Of Someone With Asperger's... 133

CHAPTER ONE

Introduction

My first book *Look Into My Eyes*, which I described as 'an autobiography through the lens of Asperger's Syndrome' shared my experiences growing up and living with Asperger's Syndrome, a high-functioning form of Autism Spectrum Disorder. In it I shared my personal experiences about what it is like to live with Asperger's, what I have found helpful, and not so helpful. I also shared my professional experiences based off of almost 20 years of working with children, teens, and adults with autism, and their parents and carers.

I felt that although I wanted it to be a 'helpful autobiography' and I had written about what parents could do to help their Asperger's child and what work colleagues, businesses and friends could do to support someone with Asperger's, and what someone with Asperger's could do for themselves to help manage different aspects of having Asperger's, all of this information was contained throughout the book and wasn't covered as fully as I would have liked because it was an autobiography with tips and strategies, rather than focusing heavily on the tips and strategies themselves, so if a reader wanted to find a tip they had to search for it and try to remember where in the book the tip was written, so I decided it would be useful to write a book of tips and strategies for those who interact with people with autism spectrum disorder, specifically Asperger's Syndrome, or high-functioning autism, and tips and strategies for people who have Asperger's Syndrome around various life areas, from work, and relationships, through to interview skills.

When I have given talks about Asperger's, I have often been approached by parents of adults with Asperger's, who have said to me that their son or daughter is very intelligent (they often tell me their child has a degree, for instance) but can't get a job because they don't do well in interviews. This always confuses me when I hear it because, to me, interviews are fine. They have a structure, and there is a process to follow; the challenge for me is remaining in the job once I have it, rather than the interview. So, in this book I will share my views and strategies around interview skills.

I will also share parenting tips for managing children and teens with Autism Spectrum Disorder (ASD) - ways that you can make the individual with ASD more comfortable. I will share tips that those with ASD of all ages can use to help themselves managing areas like sensory overload, what friends can do to help those with ASD, strategies teachers can use, and what work colleagues and employers can do to help too.

There are many strategies and ideas which are helpful in many of the different areas I'll be describing, so there will be repetition of ideas if you read all the chapters, but I still felt it was more helpful to write the different topics so that it is easy for the reader to reference, rather than write about the different tips and strategies separately and say what they are helpful for. One example of this is relaxation. Relaxation is important for parents to do, as well as for those with Asperger's, and important in many different situations, so it gets mentioned in various different chapters within the context of the chapter.

All of the tips and strategies I share are based on what has worked for me personally as someone with Asperger's, what has worked for me professionally as someone who has worked with Asperger's people of all ages, and what has worked for parents, carers and other professionals who I have worked with too.

I know that the parenting strategies work with children and teens with other conditions as well as Asperger's, like Attention Deficit Hyperactivity Disorder (ADHD), Oppositional Defiance Disorder (ODD), and angry or challenging behaviour, because I have used them myself with hundreds of children of different ages, as well as working with parents to help them use the strategies. I have also had feedback from children and teens themselves after they have improved their behaviour about what made the difference, and they report that it was changes the parents made: "My mum is now calmer and more relaxed, so I feel happier at home", or "My dad no longer shouts at me".

What is Asperger's (ASD)?

Asperger's is a collection of traits that Austrian paediatrician Hans Asperger recognised within children he was working with in the 1940's. The children appeared to have normal intelligence, but they struggled with non-verbal communication skills and didn't seem to show empathy to others. They spoke in an unusual way - often disjointed, with perhaps an odd pattern of speech, or they would speak in a very formal way, using full words and avoiding contractions (i.e., 'it does not' instead of 'it doesn't'). The children also seemed to have narrow and intense areas of interest - the only topics of conversation about which they wanted to talk.

It wasn't until 1992 that Asperger's Syndrome was used as a diagnostic term, and only in 1994 was it added to the fourth edition of the Diagnostic and Statistical Manual (DSM-IV). Asperger's has more recently been incorporated into autism spectrum disorder (ASD), as being on the 'high functioning' end of the autistic spectrum. To get a diagnosis, the psychiatrist or psychologist conducting the assessment will look to see whether the traits have been present since very early childhood, and will often want to talk to a parent or carer who can describe the birth and early years of the life of the person seeking diagnosis.

Asperger's is likely a genetic condition. There are some factors which may be related, like premature birth, and stress or illness during pregnancy. So, it is likely that someone with genetic susceptibility to Asperger's can have these genes activated by these factors. Asperger's is a lifelong, incurable condition that affects about 1 in 100 people.

Each individual with Asperger's will be affected in their own unique way. There are certain traits, but they affect each person differently. Often, the key signs are: difficulties with social interactions (including difficulties understanding the behaviours of others), an intense and narrow interest on a topic, repetitive behaviours, and in childhood there could be delayed motor development or the child may exhibit clumsiness. Often, children with Asperger's will have developed linguistically and cognitively like normal - or perhaps even had advanced development in these areas.

As a child with Asperger's grows up, a parent may begin to suspect something is different about the child due to a lack of social interaction with other children. It is important to remember that Asperger's is a lifelong condition, so a child who had many friends in primary school and nursery school, but then stays in his/her bedroom and never socialises as a teen probably doesn't have Asperger's; on the other hand, a teenager who has never really had friends through their whole childhood, or perhaps latched onto just one or two friends through their childhood may be more likely to have Asperger's.

As a parent you would be looking for clusters of behaviours. Most traits aren't necessarily all present, but there are likely to be a number of traits expressed in some form or another. So the child may grow up with good speech, but all they do is talk about themselves, which is normal for young children, but which gets less common as children grow up. Alternatively, they may feel compelled to touch specific textures, or to avoid specific textures - or even specific sounds, sights, colours or smells. Their speech may be robotic, monotonous, or repetitive. They may struggle with using or understanding non-verbal communication, but may have very good verbal communication. They may not make eye contact, something many parents and teachers then try to teach the child to do - because most people are raised to look at someone when they are talking to you, as if somehow looking at someone makes the information go into the ears better.

People with Asperger's may well absorb what they are being told better if they aren't made to make eye contact. They may also struggle to understand social or emotional situations - they may find empathising difficult. This is also something that is normal for most teenagers at some point during their development, so it is important to look at this in context with any other signs you notice.

CHAPTER TWO

Parenting Children & Teens With Asperger's

1. Your needs or theirs?

This may sound like an odd question. Many parents probably think that everything they are doing is to meet their child's needs, that they rarely get their own needs met because they are focusing so much on their child. On the surface, this may be true, but it is surprising how common it is to make decisions to meet your own needs rather than the child's, without realising you are doing so.

It could be that the child has challenging behaviour. The parent is struggling to manage this behaviour and seeks to medicate their child to help their child calm down and behave better. Yet, the child may be perfectly happy with who they are and how they are. This isn't to say poor or inappropriate behaviour shouldn't be addressed, just that you have to be mindful of the reasons for addressing the behaviour. If the medication works to control the behaviour, but makes the child feel like a zombie, and it takes away something from them, then this may not have been the best answer. The child may now be behaving, the parent may now feel things are better, and home life may be easier. This may have been a quick and easy solution, but a better solution may have been to take the longer road of helping the child with their behaviour over time, yet fundamentally they remain the same person – equipping them with the skills to manage their own behaviour.

Using the example I've just given, there is no hard and fast, right or wrong answer. I'm personally in favour of avoiding medication unless absolutely necessary. I prefer people to learn and develop skills, but this is often far more time-consuming. The main point is to help parents to look at the decisions they are making and analyse whether these decisions are focused on the needs of the child or of the parent.

So, if the parent is making the decision to give themselves an easier home life, or because they find something upsetting, then they are making the decision to meet their own needs, not the child's. An example of this could be a child who has very few friends, and spends most of their time alone. The parent struggles with this, and gets upset that their child is often alone, so they make their child attend clubs and different groups, and parties, yet the child is actually happy with the amount of socialising they do. In this case, it is the parent projecting how they feel about things in the world onto their child, and making decisions based on this, rather than recognising how their child actually feels about things in the world and what help and support they actually want.

I wouldn't want parents to feel guilty for putting their needs first at times. If a parent doesn't look after their own health, they won't be in as good a position to help their child. It is also natural for us to want to stop suffering, and so if we think someone is suffering, of course we want to stop that. Yet sometimes, what is seen as suffering by others, isn't always experienced as suffering by the person. A personal example of this is when a relationship of mine ended. My friend kept telling me I was obviously bottling up my sadness, and that this was unhealthy, that I needed to go out partying. I needed to get drunk, and I needed to sleep around. I felt I didn't need to do any of these things. Telling him this just made him believe more strongly that I was bottling up how I felt, that I should be upset and angry – I wasn't particularly. He was projecting onto me how he believed he would feel, and what he would do as a solution, and he tried to impose this onto me. He was well-meaning. He thought I must be suffering and he wanted to help me, except I'm not him; I don't experience the world like he does, and I was happy to be getting on with my life like normal.

Another area which seems common for parents to put their needs first is around school. I have worked with many parents who struggle to get their child to school. Some of these parents decide to change the school the child is attending. Sometimes this is what the child keeps saying they want; other times it is something the parent wants because they hope it will solve the problems getting them to school. Sometimes, parents will even home-school the child. There is nothing wrong with home-schooling, but when it is being done because of difficulties in getting the child to school, the parent needs to look at whether this is more about making life easier for themselves, or about helping to improve the child's education. Even when the child is saying they want to leave the school, this needs to be looked at: is it really best for the needs for the child? It is what they say they want, but are they just trying to escape a problem? I've worked with many parents who change their child's school because the child says it is what will make them behave, and they will give reasons why this will be the case, yet three or four school changes later, the child still falls back into their same patterns of behaviour after a brief honeymoon period. If the parent wants to make their child happy by removing them from the school, this is the parent meeting their desire to make their child happy, and, as a parent, their role is to sometimes make tough decisions like keeping the child in the school despite the child saying they want to leave. Leaving the school may be the correct decision, but it should be the correct decision because it is what will best meet the needs of the child: moving to a smaller school, or a more specialist school, or a school which is easier for them to get to so that they don't arrive at school feeling stressed from the journey. Or where the school and the parents feel a fresh start in a new school would be best to help the child settle in and would best help their educational attainment and wellbeing.

2. Relaxation

Relaxation is one of the most important skills someone can learn. Children feed off the emotions of their parents, even children with Asperger's, and in my experience, children with Attention Deficit Hyperactivity Disorder (ADHD) seem even more likely to feed off others' emotions.

High levels of emotion reduce the activity of the higher parts of the brain, so when someone is getting stressed, anxious, or angry (or any other strong emotion), they will see the world rigidly, and their ability to think flexibly will decrease. They will be more likely to see just one point of view, increasing the likelihood that they will make poor decisions. For parents, they may find themselves shouting at their child rather than talking calmly, they are more likely to fall into conflict, rather than a collaborative relationship.

There are many different ways you can relax, and there are a couple of different ways to look at relaxation. There are techniques which can be done to be more relaxed generally, and techniques you can do to relax when you are starting to feel emotions increasing.

Something people often say to me is they have 'no time to relax'. In my work with parents, I always advise giving time for themselves at different times of the day. So it could be that it has been a tough day at work, and after work the parent is heading to pick up a child from school. I recommend that the parent takes just a couple of minutes, or longer if possible, to relax before collecting their child. So, it could be that they park their car just around the corner from the school and do a quick relaxation technique, or meditate, or listen to the radio briefly, or whatever helps them relax, to separate and compartmentalise the day they have had at work from their time with their child or children. If they are finding things stressful at home and can't get out of the house, then is it possible to go to the bathroom for a couple of minutes, sit on the toilet, and relax before getting back to dealing with the children? When I worked in residential children's homes, this is something I used to do often, because we worked a minimum 24-hour shift and didn't get breaks, and although, like in family homes, the children would come to the bathroom and start knocking and trying to get your attention, if you timed it right you could get a couple of minutes of your own space. Often, this brief break would be enough to last another couple of hours of managing the children or teens.

General relaxation: If you take a scale (say, 1-10) then ask yourself 'on a scale of 1-10, with 10 being most stressed, how stressed are you?', and you answer that you are a 7/10, then anything else happening is very likely to tip you into unmanageable stress - just three points more stress and you will be at a 10/10. Whereas, if you have had the same stressful day, but you find a way to relax before carrying on with your evening, and you get yourself from a 7/10 down to 3/10, now the same three points only raise your stress levels to 6/10 - still less stressed than you felt before the evening. This means you will still be better able to handle situations, think clearly, and make good decisions.

Some techniques which work well for general relaxation include:

Meditation: Meditation takes two general forms, focused or mindful. With focused meditations, you are focusing in on one point and keeping your focus on that point, and if your attention strays, as soon as you recognise this you bring your attention back again. Mindfulness meditation is about being present, and not focusing specifically on any one thing. There is one warning in relation to mindfulness meditation which I don't often see mentioned, and that is that it can sometimes lead to people experiencing uncomfortable emotions. Traditionally, meditation wasn't about relaxation. Many people find it relaxing, but that isn't the purpose of it. With mindfulness meditation, the idea is to just observe ongoing experience. If that current experience is upsetting thoughts, or anxiety, or anger, then these thoughts can appear stronger because you aren't doing anything to distract yourself from them or to push them away. The idea is that you aren't attaching to the thoughts and feelings of your current ongoing experience, but if you are a beginner to mindfulness meditation, it is common to struggle to detach, and just accept that those ideas are there. With practice, you can get used to detaching yourself from the ongoing experience, and when you are detached, you enter a relaxed mind-body state because you aren't connecting with any emotions. As you develop this skill, not only will you find general levels of relaxation increasing, but you will be able to handle emotionally arousing situations better as well.

There isn't a secret formula to meditation. It is easier to do in a quiet dimly-lit place, and with your eyes closed, but this isn't essential, and it is useful if you practice using it in everyday life. So, if you are walking along, rather than talking to yourself, pay attention to many different things and practice meditative walking. As you are walking along, either focus on the walking, or just walk along being mindful - not specifically focusing on the walking, but not talking to yourself and letting any thoughts which happen to spontaneously arise drift into consciousness and back away again without addressing them or doing anything with them. This state of mind is often described as a flow-state. It is common for sports players to describe being *in the zone*, where they are just aware - not thinking about what they needed to do, or any other thoughts or ideas, they were just in the moment, reacting to the moment. This is when people often perform most optimally. Doing meditation like this and making it a part of everyday life and routine has huge benefits, it can be challenging to begin with, but, like anything else, it gets easier with practice. Another way you can meditate to relax is to use guided meditation. This can be done by just closing your eyes and imagining something. But it is easier if the guided meditation is audio recorded, so that you can listen along. This helps to prevent having to focus on what you are supposed to do.

Unlike meditation as described above, guided meditations can be done specifically to help you to relax. They usually take the form of a journey, or they have transitions of some sort. Journeys and transitions deepen the experience. People prefer different things, and there is a lot of variety, so if one thing doesn't work for you, that doesn't mean something else won't work instead. Some people respond well to pretty much any guided meditation; others like it 'just right'. For example; I prefer guided meditations spoken by a deep male voice. I like meditations with sound effects – the sound of being on a beach, if it is a beach meditation, I like meditations which are slow with plenty of silence (which also deepens the state), but someone else may prefer meditations by women, or they may not like sound effects or music in the meditation, and they may prefer something which is faster-paced. It is about trying a variety of different meditations and finding out what you like. You can also record your own.

Some meditations focus on journeys or transitions like walking along a beach, or through the woods, or travelling down a river through a jungle. Or, a transition could be something like walking through an art gallery and stepping into a painting, or walking through the woods and finding and entering a hut, or walking through the arctic and entering an igloo. Another approach is for the journey to be through your body. Generally, meditations involving your body can be good for helping with relaxation. This type of approach is commonly called progressive muscle relaxation. There are different ways you can do this, and as with other guided meditation, you can either guide yourself, or use an audio recording. Again, you will want to find a recording which has the pace and approach suited to you.

I personally prefer the focus to be from the top down, as to me, this implies going deeper, and relaxing more, whereas going from the feet up feels like it is the wrong way round. So, as I talk about it here, I will talk about the head down, rather than feet up. One approach is to focus on each part of your body in turn, and then with a relaxing deep outbreath you let your focus move down to the next part of your body. So you focus on the top of your head, taking a deep breath in, then pause a moment, then give a deep breath out and let the focus move down to your face, and repeat this all the way down to your toes. Another approach can be to tense up each body part as you focus on it, this is good if you already have some tension there, so you focus on the top of your head, scrunch up your forehead, and face, etc., hold that tension for a few seconds, then let that tension go, and let your focus of attention move to your neck, and keep repeating this all the way down through your body.

You can imagine a light passing through your body from the top of your head down, with each part of your body relaxing as the light passes through that part of the body. This could be a white light, or different coloured light, or if you wanted to it could be focusing on light passing through the chakras of your body, with the light changing and a sense of it cleansing your body as it goes.

Relaxing hobbies and interests: If there is something you do which helps you to relax, then this could be it for you. So, if you find running or exercising relaxes you, then you can make more time to do this. If listening to certain music helps to relax you, then you can find time to listen to this, and make it a time you can focus on just listening to the music, where you won't be disturbed by other things. If it is reading, then you can find time when you won't be disturbed and just focus on reading.

Self-hypnosis: Something else you can do to relax is self-hypnosis. Self-hypnosis is very similar to meditation. The main difference is that meditation traditionally isn't directive. There isn't a goal, as such; it is more about experience. Self-hypnosis, on the other hand, is usually directive - you do it for a purpose or goal. With self-hypnosis you can either do it to yourself, or, like with the meditation, you can follow along to someone guiding you through the experience. If you are doing it for yourself, then you can either follow a structured approach, like that where you begin focusing on a spot on a wall and noticing three things you can see, three things you can hear, and three things you can feel, then repeating this with your eyes closed, then opening your eyes again and noticing two things you can see, two things you can hear, and two things you can feel, then closing your eyes and repeating this, then opening your eyes and noticing one thing you can see, one thing you can hear, and one thing you can feel, then closing your eyes and repeating this. Once you have done this, you could let your focus drift to what you hope to achieve, so it could be just to relax and enjoy to relaxation, perhaps tell yourself you would like to learn how to be more relaxed in stressful situations. Then after about 15 minutes, you are likely to just drift out of the experience and open your eyes.

There are other self-hypnosis techniques you can use which are equally easy to do. Alternatively, you can listen to a guided self-hypnosis audio recording. Like with meditation, this has the advantage of allowing the listener to focus on just relaxing, rather than having to have a part of themselves trying to focus on the process, and on what they need to do. A guided self-hypnosis audio recording is also likely to be able to guide you through mentally rehearsing different situations which make you feel stressed; there are also likely to be post-hypnotic suggestions for responding differently in the future. Post-hypnotic suggestions are ideas given during hypnosis to influence behaviour after the hypnosis has ended, so there could be a suggestion that in the future, when you enter a specific situation you will feel calm and relaxed, and this suggestion will increase the chances of responding in that way in those situations. Like meditation, self-hypnosis isn't a quick fix. You are likely to need to listen to a self-hypnosis recording, or use self-hypnosis often, before you notice the benefits. The process of being hypnotised is likely to be a relaxing experience, and in my private practice I find that if someone is hypnotised, they exit hypnosis feeling very relaxed and calm. Even without suggestions for carrying on feeling relaxed, they feel far more relaxed for the rest of the day, and often into the next day, and often report that they sleep really well that night. Therapeutic change, though, often requires some time, and real-life changes, not just a change of mind, so the listener may well need to change their behaviour as well.

Relaxing in the moment: There are a number of different ways to relax in the moment depending on the circumstances.

7-11 breathing: 7-11 breathing is where you breathe in counting to seven, pause for a moment, and then breathe out counting to eleven. Breathing in activates the sympathetic nervous system – the stress response – and breathing out activates the parasympathetic nervous system – the relaxation response. With 7-11 breathing you are extending the out-breath, which encourages relaxation. In normal, everyday life, your in-breath and out-breath are about even, when you panic the in-breath is longer than the out-breath. If you check your pulse as you breathe slowly you can notice the change to your pulse while you breathe, and notice that, as you take a long breath in, your heart rate increases, and as you then take a long breath out your heart rate slows down.

7-11 breathing can be done anywhere, anytime. It is one of my favourite techniques because it can be done without anyone noticing too. I remember working with a family where the daughter had 'anger problems', according to the school and the parent. The school sent her to their in-house anger management programme for teens; they taught her to clench one of her fists when she was feeling stressed or angry, to hold her fist clenched for a few moments, before relaxing the fist and letting the tension go. Unfortunately, this wasn't the best advice; it didn't help her relax, and the other more significant issue was that she had a reputation for hitting other students when they made her angry, so when they were making her angry and they saw her clench her fist, they thought she was about to hit them! I taught her 7-11 breathing as a way she could relax without it being obvious to other students that she was doing a technique, and without anyone misinterpreting her behaviour, this had a huge impact on how she got on in school, and at home with siblings and with her mum.

Sitting down: Another way to relax yourself is to sit down, if it is safe and possible to do so. When I used to work in residential children's homes with children and teens who were often very aggressive and violent, sitting down was one of my main tactics for managing their aggression. If I felt sitting would put me at risk of harm, I wouldn't use this technique, but if the child or teen was just shouting aggressively and I didn't feel that they were likely to physically attack me, then I would sit. It is important to think about where you are sitting, so although your decision to sit down has been based on the fact you don't perceive an immediate risk of harm to yourself or others, it is always best to be sensible. So sit near an exit from the room. This way, if they decide to attack you, you can make it out of the room faster than they can get to you. Sit in a sensible location, again so that you can move quickly if you need to, so sitting on a low, soft sofa which you sink into when you sit down will be likely to help you calm down and relax, but it will also be very difficult to get out of quickly if you need to move fast. So, you may sit on an arm of a chair while you talk, rather than fully sinking down into the sofa.

There are certain actions which increase anger in yourself and others. When we are angry we want to make ourselves as big as we can, and as intimidating as we can. Often, if someone is sitting down, and they become angry, they jump up out of their seat, they get very close, and they broaden their chest, often spreading their arms too, to make themselves as large as possible. If you are dealing with someone who is angry or anxious, doing any of these intimidating behaviours is going to increase their *fight or flight* response - making them angrier, or more anxious - and if they feel trapped, it will make them more likely to want to fight to escape the feeling of being trapped.

When you feel yourself getting angry or anxious, it is helpful to take control of what you can about your behaviour. Your physical behaviour is one of those things you can control. When you sit down you may be feeling angry, anxious or scared, and you may want to stand, but by controlling yourself and remaining seated you will start to calm down as, physically, your body language isn't the body language of an angry, anxious or scared person. It is also good to talk with a calm and soft voice. Again, your voice is something you can control, so if you are talking calmly and in a relaxed manner, this will help you to relax. What's more, it will also help the person who is being aggressive or who is feeling anxious, to feel calmer and more relaxed. It is never advisable to tell the person to calm down, as this often aggravates people rather than having the intended effect.

3. Stroking and touch

Stroking can help a child with ASD to relax. Every child is different. Some may not like to be touched at all; others may like stroking from a parent, but not from other people. Some may like stroking, but only in specific locations – like being stroked on the back, or hair, or arm, but may find stroking unbearable elsewhere. You will know your own child and what they are likely to be comfortable with. The stroking may have to be a specific pressure, so stroking a child too softly can sometimes actually create more sensory input and be more uncomfortable than stroking a bit firmer, where for another child stroking firmer may be uncomfortable. So, it isn't just where you stroke which you will need to consider, but also how you stroke. Stroking has other advantages when it comes to helping a child to relax. If you stroke in time with their breathing and then slow down the stroking, this can lead the breathing to slow down as well, helping the child to relax their breathing and to calm down without having to encourage them to do so. When stroking, it is important that the parent is calm and relaxed, because this will be conveyed through the stroking. The child is likely to unconsciously pick up whether the parent is relaxed or not, and if they aren't, then the child could end up taking on some of that tension, rather than relaxing.

4. Low sensory environment

If a parent has more than one child it is often difficult to make the whole home into a low sensory environment, but it is useful if there is at least somewhere in the home which is low-sensory, for the child to go when they need to calm down. In my parenting work, I have seen environments which are too busy for children on the autistic spectrum, and I can fully understand why the child is playing up at home. I have arrived at homes with different types of music playing loudly from multiple bedrooms, a radio on in the kitchen, and a television on in the sitting room; there are dogs and cats running around everywhere, and children running around and shouting, and lights are on in all of the rooms.

This may sound like a normal family home – because, in my experience, it is – and a sterile, cold-looking family home with everything ordered and quiet would probably not be the kind of environment suited for most children to grow up in, but if a child is on the autistic spectrum, all of this (which, for most people, especially visitors who maybe don't have their own children, can seem hectic and overwhelming) is heightened. It all becomes overwhelming, and you feel like you have no escape from it. You want to stop the noise and visual stimulation, and you want to scream to banish it all. I was lucky, I grew up in the countryside. At home as a child I had to share a bedroom with one of my brothers. We had pets, including a dog, and home life was hectic, but I could go out into the woods after school and sit in a tree and relax, and come home when everyone was in bed and everything was quiet. But if the child is growing up in a town or city environment, they may not have this luxury. It may be possible in some family homes for the child to have their own bedroom, so that they have their space, or it may be possible for them to have a quiet location somewhere in the house, like in the dining room when it isn't a meal time, or in a space set up for them elsewhere in the home.

At my grandparents' house, growing up, I used to love sitting in one of the sheds. It was quite a small space, so it couldn't fit all my brothers in there with me, and it was warm and comfortable. At another house, when my grandparents moved, they had a small spare bedroom. Nan had made a long cushion which she would put on the left side of the bed against the wall to make the bed like a sofa. This room only fit a single bed and the wardrobe and drawers, with about half-a-metre of floor space between the bed and the wardrobe and drawers. This was an ideal space to relax in. All my brothers would prefer to be downstairs in the sitting room watching television or playing games, but I was happy to be upstairs in the spare bedroom. Sometimes, I would create a den underneath tables as somewhere to go that was a low-sensory environment. As a child, I didn't have headphones. I was a teenager when I got my first Walkman, and before that, I would just absorb myself in something and try to find an environment where I had low visual sensory input. I would be as far away as possible from noise as I could. I had to be creative about how to find low-sensory environments. I would sit in cupboards that were barely large enough for me to fit into, and would happily sit in there in the dark. Sometimes I would take a torch in with me so that I could read, but I wouldn't want more light than this, especially if I had been stressed or angry, because when stressed or angry, I seem to become hyper-sensitive to sensory input which can make me want to escape it even more. This is the same for others with autism; high-sensory environments are likely to increase their levels of stress or anger, making them exhibit increasing levels of challenging behaviour, or pushing them to escape or withdraw from the environment, and they may feel the need to become aggressive to achieve this.

If you can give your child a space of their own that is quiet and comfortably-lit, rather than brightly-lit, this will help them as an outlet to calm down. It could be their bedroom, or it could be another room, or just a space (a 'den') made for them in a room. This space will ideally be clear from disorganised clutter or mess. When things are messy, this draws your attention to it all and it becomes distracting, so having things neatly stacked and ordered feel more comforting than mess all over the place. I own thousands of books, and in some places

I've lived I have had books and DVDs stacked in piles on the floor due to a lack of space. To me, these are tidy because everything has an order, and I don't mind clutter as long as it is 'organised clutter', but my wife feels that everything is messy. Understandable, when she can't see the floor due to all of the piles of books! I also don't have a problem with mess I can't see. If I am looking in one specific location all the time, everything else in the room can be messy and I won't pay attention to it – or I won't care about it, because what I'm not paying attention to isn't in my mind (a common trait among those with autism). So, if a low-sensory space is set up perhaps in a corner of a room where only blank walls can be seen, then this may also work well, even if the rest of the room is quite messy.

Obviously, the ideal situation is to create the whole environment as low-sensory, with volume of the television or radios turned down, dim lights on instead of bright lights, and having people behaving in a calm, relaxed way.

5. Teaching your child social skills

Social skills are something which most people learn unconsciously as they grow up, through copying parents and older siblings. This copying isn't done consciously and systematically, yet children with autism won't do this, they will have no, or very limited awareness that there are different ways to treat people, or that different behaviour has different meaning.

An example many people may be familiar with as an analogy is when my mother started working for a food delivery company, I suddenly saw their vans everywhere. The company was well-established - it hadn't suddenly appeared overnight - but, to me, it seemed that way. I don't recall seeing the vans prior to my mum working for the company, but they had been there for years in plain sight – unseen.

Children with high-functioning autism will be good at learning, so they can be taught social skills, like teaching any other subject. Most parents won't realise how much they know about social skills and behaviour, because they do it automatically and instinctively, so it can be helpful to think about yourself and watch others, and notice what they do to get different reactions.

Some areas to teach your child are about personal space, about different facial expressions and what they mean, about what different emotions look like behaviourally, about using their voice - how different tonality and volume can be used - about focusing on the other person, rather than on themselves, and about how communication is like a dance, how what they do and how they behave influences the response they get back from others, and how others behave towards them influences how they think, feel and behave. So, saying 'please' and 'thank you' while smiling and talking calmly, will lead to people perceiving them as kind and thoughtful. Talking and behaving calmly will make others feel calmer, and so on. It is important to teach the difference between aggression and assertiveness (aggression is fighting, assertiveness is calmly giving a clear statement) and teaching about eye contact. For example, when I discovered eye contact, I learned to look through the person I was talking to and look towards their eyes for about five seconds, before looking away for five seconds, and repeating this pattern, then, as I've grown up I've learned more about eye contact, so I have more variety now, but until I learned about eye contact, I usually didn't look at someone in the eyes. I thought everyone must always be staring at each other, because I was always being told 'look at me when I'm talking to you'.

6. Routines and consistency

As with any child or teen, routines and consistency are important. With children who have autism this is even more important, because the uncertainty of not having routines and consistency can cause anxiety for the child. Even with "normal" children, a lack of routine can lead to the child exhibiting challenging and defiant behaviour. If they have additional conditions like ADHD, then poor routines and lack of consistency can make the child even more difficult to manage.

Ideally, clear routines will be in place from birth. No parent is expected to be on top form all the time, but if they are generally exerting positive parenting strategies, then their child is likely to behave better and be more manageable. If a parent hasn't cultivated an environment of consistency, as well as boundaries and consequences, and then they suddenly decide to do so, this can be a shock to the child, and many times, the child fights against the change. The most important piece of advice I would give would be to stick at it. I've worked with children and teens who have had terrible upbringings, who haven't had routines, consistency, or boundaries and consequences, who are incredibly physically violent, and - although it can be challenging - putting clear routines in place and being consistent, and ensuring there are clear boundaries and consequences has turned these children and teens around. It can sometimes take months of persistence to make the changes (often it takes longer with teens than with children), but it works. It doesn't matter whether they have medium- to high-functioning autism (it still works with low functioning autism and those with severe learning difficulties but, because they struggle to learn, it can take much longer), or whether they have behavioural problems, or attention-deficit hyperactivity disorder, etc. As a professional, it is easier for me because I'm not emotionally involved with the children or teens I'm helping, but I have also worked with hundreds of parents who have successfully implemented routines, consistency, boundaries and consequences, and turned their home lives around. In systems theory, when one part of a system changes, the whole system has to change. So, if a parent starts doing things differently, and sticks at doing things differently, the whole family system has to adjust to this and find a new "normal".

Ideally, you will have a routine for the day, so a time when everyone is expected to wake up - perhaps a routine for what someone does if they wake up early - a routine for breakfast time, for getting ready for school, for when and how to leave the home, an after-school routine, a dinner time routine, a homework routine, a pre-bedtime routine, a bedtime routine, and so on. You may have a different routine for weekends and holidays, although with children on the autistic spectrum it is helpful if this routine isn't too different, and you want consistency, so the routines are what they are; they don't change because it is halfway through the school holidays and it is easier to let the children stay in bed longer, or because it is too difficult to stick to. I had a teen who had left the children's home I was working in, and a couple of years later visited the home and spoke with the staff. He said, "Most staff here didn't care about me, but I knew you did, because every day you woke me up for school, and you kept coming and waking me up despite me throwing things at you, swearing at you and shouting at you. Even if I didn't go to school, and didn't get out of bed, right through to the last minute I should have been in school every ten minutes you were telling me I needed to be up for school." He went on: "At the time it used to really annoy me, and it became easier to just get up and go to school on the days you were working, than stay in bed and know you will be harassing me every ten minutes, but I felt you cared. The staff who tried to get me up to go to school a few times in the morning and then they just left me in bed all day without trying to get me up again, they only wanted to have an easy shift with the children in bed so that they could just sit around and drink tea, you were willing to work hard and make things difficult for yourself because you felt it was important that we get up and have an education." That teen said that he now had a job and was getting up for work on time every day, and was grateful to the trouble I went to.

You also want consistency with boundaries and consequences. So when your child or teen does something, they get a specific outcome from that, not different outcomes each time. This goes for consequences, through negative behaviours, right to positive behaviours as well.

7. Boundaries and consequences

Like with routines and consistency, boundaries and consequences are vital for parenting successfully. I have worked with many families where the parents say that their teen doesn't like boundaries, and refuses to stick to them, and yet the teen will be saying they want to join the army when they leave school, clearly demonstrating that they want boundaries and routines in place.

A lack of boundaries and consequences can lead to uncertainty for the child or teen, and a feeling of not knowing what is expected of them or how they should behave in different situations. A lack of boundaries and consequences can also lead to children and teens feeling unloved because, when they do things wrong, no-one seems to care, and when they do things right, no-one responds with positive reinforcement. This can be made worse if there are some boundaries and consequences, but they are implemented inconsistently. It is important that everyone gives the same boundaries and consequences; parents and carers should support the boundaries and consequences school staff put in place, and school supports boundaries and consequences parents and carers put in place. It is important that all those involved in the child's or teen's upbringing talk to each other to agree on boundaries and consequences, and also to agree on how they will avoid collusion and accidentally making a decision others may not. They should make sure one person doesn't take on all of a certain type of role – like when a child has been misbehaving and the child is told "wait until your dad comes home", where the father is being used as a threat of punishment, or "I'm going to tell your teachers tomorrow", or in shops where parents will say "if you don't behave, the staff will tell you off".

When I worked in children's homes, if a child wanted something and the member of staff they approached didn't already know what the consensus from the other staff was on that issue, we would always tell the child or teen that we would talk with the other staff and then let them know. If they tried to pressure us into giving an answer, we made it clear that if they wanted an answer then, it would be 'no' because we hadn't discussed it. This was a good way to ensure that a child or teen couldn't approach someone, and ask for something – like staying out later – and if a member of staff said 'no', they could go to another person, and keep going to different members of staff until they found the person who always said 'yes'. The same has applied with many families I've worked with. Children will be used to one parent being easy to persuade, and so they would pester that parent until they caved in. The advantage of having a fixed answer ("I'll discuss that with your father, and we will let you know") is that it takes pressure off the parent. They know beforehand what they will say; all they have to do then is be like a broken record and stick to saying the same thing over and over again.

One thing this teaches them is that sometimes things need planning and knowing about in advance. An incident such as where a child asks to stay at a friend's house, while the friend is there, is a prime example. The parents should stick to their guns, and even if they discuss it later and both concur that it would have been acceptable to allow it, the important thing is that they've worked as a team, and both of them know that, if the same thing happened again, they may say 'yes' straightaway because they both agree on it.

It is important that boundaries and consequences are made clear, and children have an opportunity to make their own decisions. So if a child is jumping on furniture, you don't want a parent to come in out of the blue and say "you're grounded for jumping on the furniture", you want the parent to give the child the options: "stop jumping on the furniture and sit down, you may damage the furniture or hurt yourself if you keep jumping on it" (stating what you want your child to do and giving them a chance to do it). If they are jumping on the furniture and watching television as well, you may say "if you keep jumping on the furniture the television will be turned off for the rest of the afternoon", then if they don't stop jumping on the furniture the television will be turned off. The reason 'punishments' aren't usually very good to use, is that this gave the child permission to jump on the furniture if they want to. Parents often fail to realise this. The child has been given a choice – jump on the furniture with the television off, or sit down and watch television.

Parents have often said to me that they have tried turning the television off, and it didn't make their child behave, and so they don't do the same again. Consistency is important. The child may not stop jumping on the furniture for dozens of times in a row, but they will know that what the parent says is what the parent does; one day, they may be jumping on the furniture when there is something on television they want to watch, and they know the parent will turn the television off if they keep jumping, so they stop and sit down.

If something is genuinely likely to put your child at risk, the option would be to stop them if they don't stop themselves, and in high-risk situations, you shouldn't give any options; just stop them and explain why when they are safe. So, if a child is about to run into a road, you will grab them and stop them, rather than telling them not to do it, because they may ignore you. But afterwards you will explain why you grabbed them, and explain how they should behave around roads.

The ideal option is being attentive, and using distraction. As soon as you draw attention to behaviour you don't want, you frequently get more of that behaviour. So, it is better to get a child to help with cooking or cleaning, just before the children playing nicely turns into someone accidentally getting hurt. It is much easier to do this than to tell the children to stop play-fighting. Generally, people don't like things taken away from them, so if you tell someone to stop doing something they are likely to want to keep doing it.

With consequences you want them to be as natural and logical as possible, and timely; if a child does something wrong on a Tuesday, you don't stop them doing something on the Saturday, because by the Saturday, they are unlikely to connect the behaviour they did with the consequences. If a teen goes out drinking and they are sick when they get home, then they have sick to clean up; they also don't get to lie in the next day. They still get woken at the usual time, and should be kept awake during the day. These are the natural and logical consequences of them going out drinking. Grounding them, or taking things away from them aren't necessarily natural or logical consequences.

Parents should also only set consequences they can 100% carry out. So, if you ground your teen and they just walk out of the house and ignore the grounding, then that was the wrong consequence because you haven't been able to stick to it. It doesn't matter if the consequence you choose bothers your child or not, just that you do as you say. If they carry on doing their behaviour day after day for weeks, and you keep putting the same consequence in place, and you are consistent, you will have repeatedly demonstrated that what the parent says they will do is what they do. On the other hand, if you ground a child for a month, and on day two, they go out and ignore the grounding, you can't reground them because they are already grounded for a month and stacking punishments doesn't work. Likewise, telling them they will now lose their television in their room, and then on the third day telling them they will lose pocket money, and then on the fourth day having another consequence, doesn't work either; you run out of things to do and there is no consistency. Whereas, if you ground them for an evening and do everything you can to keep them in that evening, it doesn't matter that they say it doesn't bother them. If they do the same behaviour on day two, you can always ground them for an evening again. This has the advantage that they have a sense of control of the consequences. They decide what outcome they want. If they don't want to be grounded, then they just need to do the behaviour necessary for the outcome they prefer. As a parent, all you are doing is offering them limited choices. If you have to put negative consequences in place, this is because they decided that they wanted that consequence. The consequences are timely, so as soon as possible after something has happened, and ideally 90% or more of your consequences are positive. It is very important that most of your communication with your child or teen is positive, like praise, so that even when you have to give a negative consequence, you look at how you can give positive consequences alongside it. So it could be how proud you are of how they managed being grounded, or how you understand their situation, but the consequence is what it is, or thanking them for feeling able to be honest with you if they have told you how much they hate you, etc. Also, you should regularly tell them how much you love them, and thank them for being good company when they have been, or telling them how proud you are of them when they have behaved well for someone else, or when they have done well in school. It is important that what you say is genuine and specific, and that you avoid generalising and attributing negatives – like saying "you never do as you are told", or "you always just sit down in front of the television and never help with the housework".

Consequences shouldn't mean taking away things which are positive for a child. So, if a child has an interest which is positive for them, this shouldn't be used as a consequence. Things which are positive for children are things like them engaging in sport, or socialising – especially for children who struggle to socialise. Special interests can be useful to use as something which they can do if they spend time doing other things first, but this will be different for different people. If their special interest is something like hypnosis, as it was for me, then restricting this means I would also have had 'learning communication skills' restricted, as that was how I learned communication skills. That wouldn't have been helpful to my development, so it will depend on what interests the child or teen has.

8. Acceptance and support

It is important to accept your child for who they are and how they are. They are likely to have behaviours which others find odd; they may have mannerisms which help them to relax, but are embarrassing for the parents, or lead to others making fun of them - which the parents quite rightly don't want to have happening. Naturally, their solution may be to try to stop their child behaving in these ways.

I've always stroked my hands gently between my fingers as something to help me calm down and focus internally, to escape the external world. I used to tap a lot, too. I would sit tapping my foot, or my fingers on something, or I would click retractable pens. None of these were an issue until I got my first job which involved a lot of office work, so people were around me more while I was doing these things. I would be writing with one hand, while clicking away with the other, and other staff kept complaining at me. I had to learn to stop doing this, I had to learn to relax my body and stop jiggling my feet up and down, stop tapping on tables all the time, and I don't own any retractable pens now – I stopped using them so that I would stop clicking. It is useful to know what annoys people, so although you are accepting who someone is and how they are, you can also teach them new ways of coping to replace some of the ways they currently use. What you aren't doing, though, is telling them to stop doing what they are doing unless it is inappropriate – for example, children and teens can use masturbation as a way of calming and escaping reality. Some will do this anywhere, because when they go into their own world they don't pay attention to where they are, and they don't think about others' perspectives, so pay no attention to what others may think about their behaviour. They could be in a school lesson in a classroom, or in a youth club or at home in the living room and just start masturbating; if they get told off this will come as a surprise to them because they may not even be too aware of what they were doing, and certainly not that there was anything wrong with it. So this would need addressing; it would be a case of explaining why it is wrong, and in what circumstances masturbation is okay, and what alternative behaviours they can do instead.

One thing I still do is spontaneously whistle. I have been told off in staff meetings for whistling. I've been told it is rude, yet I have been unaware at the time that I was whistling. I also pick and pull out my hair, and get absorbed in doing this and have minimal awareness that I am doing it. I *sort of* know that I am, but I feel comfortable and so don't really pay it attention, in the same way that I have some awareness that I am breathing, and when I think about it I am more aware of my breathing. I'm not totally unaware - I'm just relaxing and not really paying it attention.

So if a child feels the need to lay on the floor and scream, or to do some other behaviour which will help them but which may seem odd to others, the most helpful thing the parent can do is to accept this and support them, whilst teaching them new skills where needed. We all learn unhealthy ways of managing things, so someone could learn to eat food when they are sad as a way of relaxing and finding some calm or peace. They may not have tried to learn this, but they have learned it nonetheless. Instead, they could be taught a healthier way to relax and feel calm, rather than eating. In this way, everyone learns their own way of doing things; it is just that those with autism can learn ways of coping which others would never do, because they may think about the social element of "what would others think if I did that in public?" or "that would be embarrassing to be seen doing it". This kind of thinking stops most people developing or keeping some of these coping skills beyond early childhood.

Although there are challenges with having Asperger's, there are also strengths. These strengths should be nurtured and encouraged and focused on, rather than focusing heavily on the challenges. I have met parents who were struggling with their child's behaviour and felt they may be on the autistic spectrum, so they took them to have an assessment. There, they were told their child has autism - that it is a lifelong, incurable condition. What these parents heard was "my child has these problems and will have these problems for life". In my experience, it is rare for a parent to be told about the strengths and challenges the child will face growing up, and what they can do to help their child overcome the challenges, and nurture, develop and apply their strengths - yet this is precisely what parents should be doing. Part of this is learning about your child. For example, I worked with a parent who wanted their child to be 'sorted out'. When I asked what the problem was, the main issue was that the child never listened. I asked how they knew this, and was told the child never looked at them when they were talking to them. The child had just been diagnosed with Asperger's. The parents knew nothing about the condition, so the problem they were seeing wasn't really a problem with the child, it was a problem with not yet knowing enough about children with Asperger's. Once they learned that it was normal for children with Asperger's to not make eye contact, they explored other ways of establishing whether their child was listening or not, and they found ways to talk to their child which respected their child's individuality.

9. Space, safe place

Although it can be challenging, especially if you have more than one child, creating a safe place – a space where your child can go to calm down – is important. This space needs to be a low-sensory environment, and it needs to be somewhere they won't be disturbed. It could be their bedroom, or under the dining room table. I used to even climb into the small top cupboard in a wardrobe. The safe place is also a location the child can run off to when they need to escape. It is important that, when the child needs to escape a situation, they can do so safely, and without being chased. In my experience in children's homes, it was common for children with autism to run. If they were new to the home and hadn't yet got a safe place in the environment, they used to just run out of the building. (It wasn't a secure home, so we didn't have the doors locked.) It was dangerous for staff to follow (although they had to due to the children being vulnerable), because while they were following, the children would feel they still needed to escape, and would keep running. However, they would rarely pay attention to roads, traffic and danger, and so could get injured. It is best when the child has somewhere they can run to which is a location the parent knows as well.

Parents can engage with their child in creating the safe space, and can take the lead on how the child wants that space to be. The space needs to be comfortable for the child. It needs to be somewhere they feel safe. If the space is still noisy due to other family members, it may be that the parent comes up with solutions to this, like having noise-cancelling headphones which the child can wear in that space.

If your child is angry it is generally best not to talk to them about an incident for at least 24 hours, because even when they have psychologically calmed down they still have all the stress hormones running through their body for many hours, and so it is easy for them to be re-provoked. And because memories are state-dependant the more angry and single minded they were during the incident the less likely they are to remember details or much about it when they are calm. You can still put consequences in place, but you don't want to re-evoke the anger.

10. Encouragement, and focus on strengths

This builds on accepting and supporting your child. As well as accepting them for who and how they are, it is important to encourage them and show belief in them and their abilities, and to also encourage and show interest in any special interest they may have. It isn't helpful to be false, and to tell them they are brilliant at things they clearly aren't. You don't want to lie, but you do want to praise effort the child makes, and give as much positive praise and reinforcement as possible for every small achievement. In research on children's learning, when they are praised for success, they frequently stop doing so well when things get more challenging, and they lose interest or decide not to do things when they may not succeed. Children who are praised for the effort they put in and for doing their best, generally end up doing better and continuing to put effort in, because their reward isn't based on winning - rather, it is based on doing your best whether you succeed or not.

Focusing on strengths is also very important. Even small steps can add up to big changes in the future. There is a famous psychiatrist who had Polio as a teenager. He was paralysed from the neck down. One day, he was sat at home, tied to a rocking-chair, while his family carried on with what they had to do (farming and chores). As he sat in the chair, he closed his eyes and longed to be outside with his family, then he noticed the rocking-chair began to rock. He recognised that, somehow, his thoughts led to unconscious movements in his paralysed body so he decided to see if he could use this to treat his paralysis. He stared at the back of one of his hands and vividly imagined what it would feel like to climb the tree in the garden - how his fingers would move to grasp the tree, how his wrist would move, how his whole arm would move. Then, he noticed twitches in the back of his hand. He kept at it, day after day, week after week, until his fingers started moving in one hand. Then his hand started moving, then his forearm, then his whole arm, and over a period of many months, he managed to be able to stand and walk, and talk. It all began with twitches in the back of one of his hands, and giving himself positive feedback, and focusing on the 'strength'. He thought, if he could have movement in the back of his hand, he could have movement in his fingers; if he could move his fingers he could move his wrist; and if he could move his wrist he could move his arm. He didn't focus on the rest of his paralysed body, he knew it was paralysed, but that wasn't what he wanted, so he had to focus on building on the strengths.

I'm passionate about solution-focused therapy. Some people I meet, though, think it is an approach which ignores the problem. It isn't. It is an approach which tackles the problem head-on, rather than hanging around, focusing on what is wrong (which clients usually already know). It is an approach which focuses on what needs to change to get what you want, how you can make those changes, and what small parts of what you want are already happening; the rationale is that it is easier to build on these, than to start from scratch. This kind of mindset is really helpful for parents to use with their children. They can find what needs to be achieved – like certain skills, or ways of managing situations, then find what they are doing already in that direction, and build on this, giving plenty of praise and encouragement to keep them moving in the right direction.

The same psychiatrist I just mentioned was a master at building on people's strengths. He had an elderly client whose husband had died. She wanted to learn to read and write now she was on her own; she had to deal with the things her husband had dealt with all the years they were married. She had never learned to read or write. Before seeing this therapist, she had seen many other people, both teachers and therapists, and none of them had any success.

The therapist, Dr Milton Erickson, knew she had grown up and lived on a farm all her life, so he asked her to draw a pitchfork, to draw a barn, to draw carts, to draw many things which were familiar to her. He then took her drawings and showed her that the barn she drew looked like an A, that the top of the pitchfork looked like an I, that the bottom of the pitchfork turned on its side looked like an E, turned the other way looked like a 3, and sticking in the ground looked like an M, and upside down looked like a W, and the wheels of the cart looked like an O. It didn't take him long to teach her to read and write. She had 'written' all of these letters when she drew different things on a farm, and, with these letters she had 'written', she was now also learning to read. Erickson said all he did to help her was to find something she knew well. He used that as the starting place to scaffold her new learning.

11. Getting their needs met

Children with autism spectrum disorder may struggle to get their needs met. They may need help to learn how to get their needs met in healthy ways. When I was a teenager, I became a very heavy drinker. At my peak, I was drinking about 18 pints per night. I did this because it was something to do. I was able to hide behind the glass, and be drinking all the time. It is the same as people making themselves look busy in work when a manager is walking past. If I didn't have a drink to my mouth, I probably would have been expected to engage in conversation. I would have had to figure out what to do with my hands, where to look, and generally socialise – or worse still: get up and dance (which I did end up doing a couple of years into attending clubs, but I had to learn how I was supposed to dance before being prepared to actually do it). With a drink, I could always be looking at the drink. I could have my hands on my lap, and frequently reach for the glass, pick it up and drink, or move it. I didn't used to like talking to bar staff, so I would arrive early and get a drink, and then the next five or six people to arrive would buy a round, and so I wouldn't have to buy another drink until drink eight, by which time I was drunk and didn't feel so nervous asking for drinks at the bar.

I have met many teens and adults with Asperger's who have found unhealthy ways to get their needs met, or who are depressed, or who suffer with anxiety or other conditions because they haven't found ways to do this. Parents can help, and the earlier they start helping, the better, because there aren't classes in schools teaching how to get your needs met. I know someone who suffered with depression when they were in school and they didn't understand what the horrible feeling was that they felt. They had no words for it, and they didn't know other people had felt that way as well. It wasn't until they became an adult that they learned they were depressed when they were younger, and that they had been depressed as an adult as well. The difference was that, as an adult, because they knew what was wrong, they were able to get help and learn skills to move on, and to reduce the chances of them feeling depressed in the future. They told me they wished that they had been taught about depression and anxiety in school, and about how to avoid becoming depressed, and how to manage anxiety.

Although children on the autistic spectrum don't like too much choice and don't like uncertainty, they are human like everyone else, and so they have the same needs. One of these needs is to have a sense of control. If others always make decisions for them, then they will feel like they have no control over things in their life, so offering a couple of choices gives them the opportunity to have control over the decision. They will have a need to feel like they belong, yet they may be very different from siblings and other family members, so it is important to find a way of helping them feel like they belong. They will have a need to have a sense of status and achievement. This can often be achieved by helping them to recognise what they are good at, and how they are progressing and improving.

There are many innate emotional needs which need to be met in healthy ways. If they aren't met in healthy ways they may well be met in unhealthier ways, so parents can help to foster healthy, positive routes to doing this, but it is important to remember that the level at which needs have to be met vary from individual to individual. The parent may want to have an active social life to meet the need for having a connection to others, yet the child may be happy to see other people just a couple of hours per month. If the parent tries to force them to see people more frequently, the child is likely to resist this and may withdraw and want to see people less; the parent needs to look at how different needs need to be met from the child's perspective.

12. Managing siblings

A child with autism can often have a huge impact on siblings. Parents need to still spend plenty of time with the other siblings and teach fairness, rather than sameness. Many parents have told me that their children will say it is unfair their autistic child is getting certain treatment, whether it is having a space of their own at home, or they get to go to a 'special school', or they don't have to go to school for so many hours. Depending on the age of siblings, they can see different treatment as being unfair. Parents can explain about each of them being treated equally and fairly, rather than being treated the same.

Some siblings may be young carers, having to offer support to looking after their autistic brother or sister, so they may need plenty of praise. Parents can look at ways to ensure there is time for their non-autistic children to just be children.

If it looks like conflict may happen, it is useful to get used to the common triggers and plan how to handle them. One good way of handling them is to use well-timed distraction or diversion, like calling one of the children to help with cooking at a moment when you know things are likely to escalate if you don't intervene, and to make sure there is clear age-appropriate communication with the children. So, if it is very difficult to move the child with autism from the room and so the parent is always telling the other children to leave the room, and they see this as unfair, then it is helpful to explain to them why this is being done, and to make sure that it doesn't seem like a punishment to them. If other siblings bully the child with autism then this would need to be addressed with clear boundaries and consequences, as well as good communication about it being wrong, why it is wrong, and what the expectations are on how they should be behaving.

One thing many parents experience is disappointment from their non-autistic children when they were looking forward to a trip out somewhere, but because of an incident happening suddenly with no notice, the trip doesn't happen and they have to stay home. A parent can't change what has happened, and can't guarantee that an incident won't happen, so can't make any clear promises to their children, and it is important not to make promises unless you are very confident that what you are promising will happen. But a parent can look at what options they have, and can make a contingency plan. They could plan that one parent, or a grandparent or other family member, could take the other children while one parent stays home with the child with autism, or the parent could take the children while a friend or family member stays and looks after the son or daughter staying behind.

13. Pets and animals

Most children with autism spectrum disorder get on very well with animals, and seem to have a closer affinity with animals than they do with other people. There are a few, however, who may have other conditions as well or negative life experiences, and who may display violence towards pets and animals. This is reasonably rare. For most people on the spectrum, pets and animals are helpful. Stroking animals can be very calming and relaxing, and give a feeling of safety. Dog walking can give the child a chance to get some fresh air and exercise. Having pets can teach responsibility, and help to teach about forming relationships.

Animals are far easier to understand; they generally display one message in any communication that needs deciphering. Learning to approach and engage with animals can teach about learning to approach and engage with different kinds of people, because how you use your body language and voice is very important with animals, and for some reason, when communicating with animals, this seems to be more naturally understood, whereas when communicating with other people this often gets overlooked. Perhaps much of the focus goes onto trying to say the correct thing, rather than to do the correct thing.

14. Food, clothing, and hair

Many issues with children on the autistic spectrum centre around food, clothing and their hair. This is often because they are hyper-sensitive to physical sensations, and they like certain textures. They may be fussy eaters - not because they like or dislike certain foods, even if they say this is the case. It may simply be that they don't like the texture or sensation of eating certain foods. For example, I like food to be sloppy. I don't like dry foods. I generally don't like mixing foods. If I eat a steak, I want just a steak. I don't want sauce on it. I don't want to mix beans and steak together on a fork to eat it. I want to eat the chips with mayonnaise – because chips are dry, and if I don't have mayonnaise then I will eat the chips with the beans, then I eat the beans, then, finally, I eat the steak. This is the same for all meals. I will eat the items on the plate in an order, I will try to make everything I eat have the correct texture and consistency. I don't appreciate food, and the flavours of food particularly, and I will never feel that something was a 'lovely meal'. It is just food.

If a child says they don't like a certain food it can be helpful to find out why, by asking what they don't like about it – rather than "why don't you like it?". For example, it could be that vegetables are often served quite hard, rather than overcooked as they may prefer them. Or a food may have a consistency which sticks it to the roof of their mouth, or gets in their teeth, or seems like it has bits in it. So, it then becomes a case of looking at how the foods can be presented right for the child so that they eat as wide a diet as possible, rather than deciding they only eat one thing – say, burgers and chips – and refuse to eat anything else. It can be hard work, but they need to get used to eating a diet rich in variety, and this is easier to help them do, the younger they are.

They may also expect things to have certain patterns to them, so they will eat foods in certain orders on the plate, and may not eat the food if it is just piled up on top of each other, so how the food is presented is important. Having the child involved in food preparation can help with this, but at the same time I have made pasta salads for children and teens who don't eat most of the ingredients, yet they love the pasta salad. If they see how it is made and what goes into it, they refuse to eat it, even though they like the taste of it. They will tell me they don't like this ingredient, or that ingredient, yet those same ingredients are in each pasta salad I make.

Another issue which can happen with food, and which definitely happened with me, is that food can be a way of constantly appearing occupied. So if I am eating, I'm not necessarily expected to talk or engage in conversations with people. All I have to do in a social situation is not stop eating, and I can get through the whole event without talking to anyone.

If a child is using food as an unhealthy solution to a problem – like solving anxiety of socialising, by non-stop eating so that they don't have to socialise, then this needs to be addressed, and the parent needs to help their child find healthy solutions, such as learning social skills, or learning relaxation techniques.

Clothes can present many problems. As a child, I hated school socks. I struggled to manage to get them on; they often turned around on my foot so that the heel part of the sock was on the top of my foot, and they always felt uncomfortable and drew all of my attention to them. They would somehow manage to always fall down during the school day, and be clumped up uncomfortably in my shoes. My shoes always rubbed my ankles and the top of my foot; school jumpers over shirts would seem to twist the shirt tight and uncomfortably around my arms; the jumpers would itch; shirts and ties would feel like they were strangling me; and trousers would itch and rub on my legs like having sandpaper rubbing my legs all day. Many children with autism will most likely have similar experiences, or perhaps even worse than this.

Although it can take a very long time, it is good to try to find clothes the child feels comfortable in, and once you find certain materials they like, and specific items of clothes they like, try to get these items in the future. It is common to want to get items for school that the child can grow into, because children grow so quickly that you want each item of clothing to last as long as possible. But if an item of clothing is too loose, then it can be uncomfortable and distracting, and if it is too tight it can be uncomfortable and distracting. So a parent has to weigh up what is the right item for the child, whilst also thinking about how long the item is likely to be worn. Depending on the child, there may be items which can be worn under clothes to help them feel comfortable, like a t-shirt under the shirt. Only the child will know what they feel are suitable textures. When I go into clothes shops with my wife, she will find items she thinks I will like, and will say "check out how soft this is". I'll feel it and think it is like touching sandpaper. The child may also have a preferred weight to the clothing as well. Differently-weighted clothing will hang differently, and feels different to wear.

Some children may want to not wear any clothes. This may not be a problem at home, but when out and about, and in school, this isn't generally socially acceptable. They will need to be helped to find clothes they can wear when they need to, and perhaps told that they only need to wear the clothes in these certain situations. Negotiating - telling them in what situations they can be free from the clothing - is likely to have a better outcome than trying to dictate to the child just one way of being. Unfortunately, there isn't any simple answer I know of to make a child get used to uncomfortable clothing. Wearing something frequently can help, because anything which is in your attention constantly and unchanging, you stop paying attention to it, so people who wear glasses will forget they have glasses on their face. Likewise, a child wearing something regularly and not moving too much, may get used to certain items of clothing. Generally, the best that can be done is to help them to be able to manage how they feel in certain clothing, and to find items and materials which are right for them. This will help hugely in the future, as they will grow up knowing what clothes to buy in order to aggravate them least. It may help them to find solutions like undergarments so that certain clothing isn't directly on their skin. I wear almost the same items every single day; once I find something which is comfortable to wear I will buy more than one of them, or just keep wearing and washing the same item until it wears away. Then I will buy the same item again, and do the same again. One of the most important things with this, with food, and with haircuts, is to help them to be able to remain calm, so that they don't associate anxiety or anger with these things, as this could have a negative impact later in life.

Having a haircut is another problem area which seems common among those with autism. I know I hate having my haircut, and once I've found somewhere to cut my hair, I want to go back to that exact same place every time. I want to see the same hairdresser, and ideally I want to be alone in the shop. When I used to walk-in off the street at a hairdresser's, I used to walk past repeatedly until I saw there were no customers inside. Only then, would I enter and ask for my haircut. Then, I would face the stressful task of trying to ask for the hairstyle I want, and then having the hairdresser trying to make small talk, and all the time worrying that they may not follow the exact instructions I gave them about how I wanted my hair styled. I used to put off getting my hair cut, and would have it cut once to twice per year, maximum. It would take me weeks to finally go for the haircut, and perhaps days of walking backwards and forwards outside the venue before finally entering. Now, I book online. I still get stressed by the whole thing. I still worry about whether they will do my hair right. I still have to manage the hairdresser when they try to make small talk, and all the other issues. But I do it every few months, because I have to if I want to look presentable.

I don't know of any autism-friendly hairdressers, but here is my view on what one would look like… Each customer would be separated off with partitions from the others, where the hairdresser is patient, and willing to change what they have done if they haven't cut the hair properly. They would also take the lead from the client about whether to talk or not, asking whether the client would like to talk about anything, rather than asking what you had been up to, or what you will be doing later. They would following any answer up with "would you like us to talk about that, or something else, or would you prefer not to talk?"

One of the issues with having a haircut is the sensation of the cut hair falling on to your face, and tickling or itching. Most hairdressers don't do anything about this - they don't even seem to notice this has happened - and you are sat there under a robe normally, which is difficult to move your hands out from, so you can't wipe your own face. And then there is the loud buzzing of the clippers, and the tickle on your neck. Everyone will have a pressure which works for them, so some people will want the hairdresser to be firmer, so that they don't have the soft tickling; others may find the hairdresser too firm and need them to be softer.

As a parent, the most important thing is to find out what it is about going to the hairdresser (or having the parent do things to their hair) they don't like. For example, as a child, I always had my haircut at home by my mum, and she would always give me a fringe, but this would tickle my forehead and be very uncomfortable and irritating. This contributed to my dislike of having my haircut, because it was so uncomfortable. Even now, when my hair grows to a length where a fringe naturally starts forming, it tickles and I will spend lots of my time focusing on it and getting angry with it because of how irritating it is.

15. Supporting your child or teen if they are experiencing bullying or discrimination

If your child is being bullied or discriminated against, they may not realise; even if they do, they may not care. Yet whether the child realises or cares, if the parent knows about it, they will want to stop the bullying or discrimination.

Like with any child, it is important that what the parent does is child-led, not parent-led, unless there is a clear safety reason for taking action. But, generally, you want the child to be helped to learn how to handle the situation themselves in the future. If they speak about being bullied or discriminated against, the parent's response should be to listen and sympathise, and to then ask if there is anything the child would like them to do. And if the child doesn't understand what you mean, and what sort of things you may be able to do, then the parent can state what they can do to help. The child may well have just wanted to offload, or they may want advice on what they could do. They may, indeed, want the parent to do something. But it is down to the child to feel that they are making the decision over what they want. When parents jump in too quickly, they take away a child's developmental opportunity, and with children on the autistic spectrum who struggle with social interactions, it is important to teach them and support them in developing and using their social skills as the ideal first option. The parent can then step in if the child needs help, so that the parent is helping the child to solve the problem first, and only stepping in if they are needed.

16. Collaborative communication

Anytime there is a divide created there is an increased risk of conflict. So if a child says "you love my brother more than you love me", the parent has a number of ways of handling this, they can respond by saying "that isn't true, I love you both equally", or they can respond with something like "what is it I do which makes you think that?" and "for you to know I love you both equally, what would I have to be doing differently?".

These latter responses are examples of collaborative communication. The parent comes alongside the child, and accepts that the child's perspective on reality is valid and true as far as they see things, whereas the first response opposes the child's views. The first response is more likely to lead to an argument because it doesn't respect that the reality someone has is as real to them, as your reality is to you. So, if a child believes their parent loves their brother more than them, then to them, this is their reality. They will have a good reason for believing this. The parent may know this to be false, but that doesn't change the child's experience.

The latter responses ask questions which find out why the child has the perspective they have. It is important to use 'why' as infrequently as possible, as it isn't a helpful way of getting information - it often gets opinions rather than facts. On the other side of the coin, 'what, when, who, and how' questions get facts. So, asking "what is it I do which makes you think that?" can lead to answers about what behaviours they are observing which give them that perspective. Asking "what would I have to be doing differently?" will lead to answers about behaviours you need to do differently. Thus, these two questions help you know how what you are doing is being perceived, and what you need to be doing differently to solve the situation.

I worked with a family where the child told the parent they never listen. The parent argued back, stating that they do listen. This argument went on and on, getting heated, and remaining unresolved. When the parent asked what it was that made the child think that way, the child replied that they are always busy - like washing up or cooking - when they tried to talk, or looking at their mobile phone. The parent did these things, indeed, but felt he was multi-tasking and listening; clearly, this wasn't how the child saw it. So, the solution, to make the child feel listened to, was that when they spoke to their parent, the parent would stop what they were doing and engage fully with the child. And if they couldn't stop, they would stop briefly to explain to their child that they were busy because they had to get dinner done, for example, and that the child could either talk to them while they cooked, or if they wanted full attention, there would be a specified time later when they would be free to talk.

You want as much of the communication with your child to be positive and collaborative, where you come alongside them, rather than opposing them. This isn't always possible, but it is something to aim for. So, even if the child is being abusive towards you, you can still thank them for being honest with you, as well as addressing how that isn't the way to communicate with people. In such a way, you are addressing problems, and poor behaviour, whilst also coming alongside the child and looking at finding solutions and a way forward from this point; you are being humble enough not to get defensive when attacked, but to accept that, from their perspective, they believe they are right.

17. Seeking autism spectrum disorder diagnosis

When seeking a diagnosis for your child or teen, there are some important things to remember. It isn't just a case of going to the GP and asking them to make a referral for your child to have an assessment. You will need to say what behaviours your child does and what traits they have that make you think they may have autism. You will have to say why it is you want the diagnosis. It is common in most places that they don't diagnose just because a child has autism; rather, they only diagnose if the child is being affected by having autism, and where a diagnosis would be helpful. So if the child's needs can be met, and behaviour can be managed without the need for a diagnosis, then this is usually preferable to labelling a child. There are many people on the autistic spectrum without diagnosis who cope fine, and who don't need a diagnosis to get additional support. You will also have to demonstrate how the child's behaviour and traits happen in all areas of their life – home, community, and school, and describe how the behaviour and traits have been there pretty much since birth.

All of this information needs to be on the letter the GP sends to the child and adolescent mental health services (CAMHS), or whichever organisation diagnoses in your area. In many areas, if they receive a letter from a GP just saying this parent would like to have their child assessed for autism spectrum disorder, without supporting information, they will reject the letter. Likewise, if there is only evidence of difficulties in the family home, and school is fine, or vice versa, then they are likely to reject the referral. If they don't display the behaviours or traits in certain situations and you think you know why this is, then this will need to be put down as well. It could be that they attend a school where they are in a very small class, and the school has put in great support - the staff are very good at understanding children on the autistic spectrum, and they have great boundaries, structure, flexibility to deal with issues when they arise, etc.

The assessment will usually consist of some detailed questionnaires to fill out, and sometimes a phone consultation with the parent, which may conclude as either positive (a diagnosis on the autistic spectrum), or negative (a conclusion, from the information given, that it doesn't sound like your child is on the autistic spectrum). Alternatively, they may arrange a face-to-face consultation with the parent and child. Sometimes they don't do a phone consultation, and other times they ask if you mind them talking with other professionals like the school, and they may ask for an educational psychologist to see your child in school.

Seeking a diagnosis can be a long process, and sometimes parents can feel they are being treated as though they have been a bad parent. What is often suggested is to have parenting support, even before diagnosis - not because you are a bad parent, but

but there was no obvious support in place once the course had started. One issue was poor structure and clarity. I wanted clear, easy-to-access information about things; I wanted to know what was expected of me and by when; and I wanted other students to be as dedicated and put in as much time and effort as me. I would get the weekly assignment and complete everything on the same day. I would then expect to interact with other students in the forums all week (which was an essential and unavoidable part of the course), but what happened was other students left everything to the last minute, and joined the forums towards the end of the last day when it was too late for me to interact meaningfully in the remaining time. The webinar call-ins would spend the first 30 minutes with people trying to get the software working, and once it was working, it would crash at one or more of the instructors' ends, and we would spend so much time waiting with people trying to fill the time making small talk. Or, worse, we would have to interact with each other. This was even worse when their voices and faces didn't sync up well and I couldn't read and understand properly what they were communicating.

Even when I dropped out, they weren't attentive to my needs. They contacted me a couple of months after I dropped out to say my assignment was late, without seeming to notice that even though there were probably fewer than 20 of us on the course, I hadn't been there for months. I wasn't on any of the call-in's, and I hadn't submitted any work, or taken any of the tests for weeks, and when I was there I was becoming increasingly blunt and assertive in the webinar calls, and when I said why I had dropped out - despite this being one of the most important things I had ever done with my life - the

CHAPTER THREE

Teaching Those With Asperger's

Everything in this section applies to teachers, and teaching establishments who offer education to all age ranges and in all forms, from distance-learning, to based in a primary or secondary school, or college or university. An example, even as an adult, of the importance of how teachers and educational establishments need to consider how they teach those with Asperger's is my experience as an adult when I started a distance-learning degree. To me it was one of the most important things I had ever done; it meant so much to me to do this degree. I had worked really hard to get on the course, and within a couple of months I had quit because it wasn't being run in an Asperger's-friendly way. I struggled to cope with how it was led, and my default setting is that I reach a point where I give up and walk away, never to try again.

They knew I had Asperger's, and had processes in place to talk to me before the course started about my needs, has – for one reason or another – not been supported consistently. They will want to rule this out first. I know parents often feel frustrated when they are told to get parenting support before coming back to see if a diagnosis is required, but the reality is the parent will now have the skills to manage their child, regardless of whether they end up being on the autistic spectrum or not.

It is useful to join a parenting group for parents of children or teens with ASD, and ideally where parents have an active role in the group and can share advice and knowledge. Avoid groups where they become all about complaining about services, or each other's children. You want the group to be positive and focused on how to solve issues that are being faced, not just dwelling on the issues themselves.

You can also liaise with the school for support through education, health and care plans, and other support the school and other professionals may be able to offer. It is also worth talking to a benefits advisor about what benefits you may be entitled to, to help with your child.

because there are things they may not know or do currently which could improve home-life, and these things work with most children, both on and off the autistic spectrum, but particularly when done consistently with a child on the autistic spectrum. When I used to work as a parenting support officer, the first thing CAMHS would often do when they contacted parents upon receipt of a letter asking for an assessment, was to give the parents my details and tell them to use the parenting service. Parents contacting me were often frustrated saying they didn't want parenting support, they wanted their child helped; they didn't know that the parenting concepts used were the same whether the child has autism, or ADHD, or ODD, or challenging behaviour, or no issues at all. In reality, the only thing that is different is tailoring the way the parent applies these concepts to their own child, and being prepared to put in hard work.

For parents where there has also been additional factors, like domestic abuse at home, or evidence of prior parenting issues (for example where the parent was depressed, or has perhaps had an alcohol or drug problem, or where trauma may have happened to the child, like the death of a close grandparent), then the parent may be asked to seek parenting support first to ensure the parenting approach is at a high standard. Then, if the child has other issues, they may recommend the child talks to someone about this, or addresses it in some way. After doing all this, they then come back about the diagnosis, because it may not have been autism, it could have been due to these other issues instead, where a child response wasn't supportive, it was that I should have sought help, and that I had a day or so to get my assignment in. If it wasn't, I would definitely be off the course. My experience led to my decision that I would never try to get further education again, despite a dream of mine since childhood: to be educated to PhD level.

So, I didn't feel they were supportive of me, or that they were attentive or responsive to my needs. There was a lack of clarity, too. Before I started the course, I had been told that it was a one-year course which could be reduced by up to 50% of the course based on prior learning and experience, so it could be completed in as little as six months. When I paid to take the course, I couldn't find the details about its length, so a few weeks in, I enquired and they said it had changed now to taking a minimum of 18 months to complete.

Once the goalposts were changed and I had gone from something I thought would take six months or so of intense studying, to three times that amount, all my motivation was gone. So, from the start, there was uncertainty, which is a quick way of pushing me to escape the situation. With that in mind, everything in this section is written not just to help teachers of children and teens, but also to hopefully encourage adult education teachers to look at what they offer and how they can make sure they and their workplace are autism-friendly to help people achieve, rather than quit.

1. Relaxation

Relaxation is one of the most important skills someone can learn. People feed off the emotions of others, so students will feed off the emotions given by the teacher, and, likewise, teachers can feed off the emotions of the students.

High levels of emotion reduce the activity of the higher parts of the brain, so when someone is getting stressed, anxious, or angry (or any other strong emotion), they see the world rigidly, their ability to think flexibly decreases, they are more likely to see just one point of view, and this increases the likelihood that they will make poor decisions.

If the student is stressed, anxious or angry, they will develop black-and-white thinking, and be likely to just see their perspective, believing that they are right. They are likely to see any challenge to this as a conflict which someone has to win, and they are likely to fight to try to win if they are feeling angry, or to escape the conflict or the situation if they are feeling anxious. Ultimately, if the teacher continues to confront them, then they will feel like they have to fight to escape.

For adult students with Asperger's who find themselves stressed, anxious, or angry, the same applies; they will see the world even more black-and-white than usual. They may fall into a conflict relationship with others who think differently. Depending on what skills have been learned about how to behave socially, the adult may try to remain quiet, or may even try to walk away if they are angry, rather than arguing with others, and if the situation is causing them anxiety, stress or anger, then they may decide to leave the situation for good.

This is something which has happened to me a number of times, where there is uncertainty in a situation, or where the situation is overwhelming or causes me stress in some way. While in that highly emotional state, I will walk out, never to return, rather than remaining and experiencing the stress. Luckily, over the years, I've improved my ability to relax, so I do this less frequently now.

In school, if other students tried to give me the bumps, or tried to 'bundle' me for fun, I would suddenly feel a surge of anxiety. With the rapidly-increasing anxiety, I would quickly enter a fight-or-flight state of mind, where I would do whatever I had to, to prevent it from happening. My first instinct was to run, but if I was grabbed by anyone I would do whatever I had to do to break free and prevent the person from grabbing me again. I had no problem with the idea of trying to break fellow students' arms or legs, or trying to seriously hurt them in some other way. To me, in that state of mind, this was the only option I could see to ensure the thing which would cause me high levels of anxiety didn't happen. My mindset was to escape the threat first, or neutralise it as a backup plan. In my professional work, I have seen this happen with children and teens in school who have ended up excluded. Often, people say that their behaviour seemed to come out of nowhere – it was an 'over-the-top reaction'. When I was a child, I didn't have the insight about my behaviour that I do now. I didn't know what the rush of feelings was, or how to put any of it into words. I have also seen this with children and teens I've worked with, where they react a certain way and can't explain themselves. This can naturally be frustrating for adults who want to know *why* they behaved in a certain way. What I often say to adults – parents or teachers – is that it isn't important to try to get the *why* from the child; listen to *what* happened and observe the pattern. Then you can find out *why*, even if the child or teen doesn't know why themselves.

As a teacher, it is important to be relaxed with students, to be down at their level when talking to them. Don't worry about whether you get eye contact, or whether they appear not to be listening, because perhaps they are doodling, or fidgeting, or exhibiting a strategy to help them relax – often *stimming*, giving some form of self-stimulation which focuses and absorbs their attention, or maybe saying something. Stopping them doing these things will increase their stress levels, just like telling a smoker who smokes to manage their stress that they are no longer allowed to smoke. If they haven't learned alternative ways to manage stress, then stopping smoking - which is their therapy for stress - is going to be difficult to do. Thus, you can help to teach the student how to relax and focus, and as they learn and get used to using new strategies, they will stim less. Being alongside the student and both focusing on a shared point is more helpful and relaxing, than sitting opposite the student and trying to look them in the eyes.

Breathing slowly and calmly, with your in-breath being longer than your out-breath with help you to remain relaxed, as will relaxing, quietening and lowering the pitch of your voice, and relaxing your body muscles, letting your arms and shoulders relax.

2. Attentive and responsive to the individual

Children on the autistic spectrum, just like children who are shy, often won't speak out in class. It could be that they don't know how to speak out and so choose not to, or that they play up to get attention rather than speaking out, and this gets viewed at poor behaviour. Either way, the child still hasn't received the help they were after. Or they may just not think about saying anything. This was me in school. It didn't usually cross my mind to ask for help; I just sat quietly trying to get through the lessons. If I got stuck and did want help, I didn't know how to ask for it, so I didn't. I always wanted the teachers to be mind-readers and somehow just come to me and offer me help.

So, it is important to be attentive to recognise the signs of a child who is trying to get attention without drawing attention to themselves, and being responsive to this. All of my school reports for each lesson, and each year, said that I needed to ask for help more, that I needed to interact and engage in class more. Teachers were clearly noticing that I needed help enough to write it in my yearly reports, yet they didn't seem to notice enough to proactively come over to me and offer me help. They were waiting for me to ask.

3. Structure and clarity

Schools are generally great places when it comes to structure and clarity. You get a timetable, so you know what you should be doing, and where and when, and classes usually have specific things in terms of content. What's more, the class will be taught in a structured way. But there are times when things aren't so structured. Physical education can be a challenge; you know when and where you are having the lesson, and you may well know what the lesson will be about, but if it is team sports, you don't know who will be picked for what teams, and whether you will be picked last. There is also always a sense of uncertainty about changing afterwards, because you never know what other children are going to do: is someone going to run over and pull down a towel you have wrapped around you as you change? Is someone going to try to bully you in the changing room for being different? Or try to soak you and your things in the showers leaving you to have to go through the rest of the school day laughed at and wet, or wearing spare clothes which irritate, and aren't yours? So, it is helpful for children with Asperger's to be told how lessons will go, and to find solutions to worries they may have.

If supply teachers are used, then at the earliest opportunity this needs to be communicated to the child to let them know the new structure and routine. It may be that they don't feel comfortable going into the lesson because of this, so alternative arrangements can be made, like having them do the work in another room, or in the library.

Having structure around what to do if they are running late to a lesson, or if they suddenly feel anxious, and clearly building up to times when routines and structures change, like perhaps around exam times, or near school holidays, or non-uniform days, and making sure all of this is clearly explained and checked with the child to ensure they understand, and to ensure there is structure and clarity between what happens at home and at school, and also in the transitions between home and school.

4. Calm and supportive

Most teachers will already be calm and supportive, but with a someone with Asperger's, this is very important. The view that children with Asperger's don't have feelings or emotions is incorrect. What is correct is they are usually hyper-sensitive to feelings and emotions, just like other sensory experiences, but they don't necessarily understand what the feelings are and can quickly get overwhelmed by them, just like being overwhelmed by sounds, light, movement, or physical sensations, and they can want to escape this overwhelming sensory input. It is like sitting in a quiet room and then suddenly having someone turn on multiple audio players with loud crashing, screeching music, all playing different songs, none of which go together.

Having a teacher who seems calm and supportive and on your side can mean so much and be so helpful. The child is more likely to feel comfortable talking to them when they need help. When the world feels a very overwhelming place, you need a calming presence to help you to focus and centre yourself, almost like a rock in a sea of noise.

5. Clear explanations and clarification

Students with Asperger's can sometimes think they understand something, yet find later that they didn't. In my first year of secondary school I had to make a bridge out of cotton and spaghetti that would hold as much weight as possible in Science class, and then write what I did. Those were the instructions I was given. I made the bridge then wrote in my Science exercise book: 'I made a bridge out of cotton and spaghetti'.

My science teacher asked me if I'd had help making the bridge. I said no, explaining that I didn't think my parents would know how to make a suspension bridge, or that it would be the type of bridge likely to hold the most weight. She then asked me questions about my bridge, all of which I answered, and ended by saying that she questioned whether I made the bridge because what I wrote showed no understanding of how to build the bridge I built, or why. She told me that everything I told her needed to be written down. I said the question didn't ask me to write all that down. She explained that I should always imagine someone being curious and asking me lots of questions about what I had done and why, and everything I should write down everything I would answer, that I would probably write too much at times doing that, and it may not all make sense, but cleaning up the writing can be learned. I just need to make sure I get it all down on paper first.

This had a huge impact on my school life, I definitely did better at writing things down after being told this. But the original problem was that the explanation wasn't clear. This is a common problem, especially when questions have been worded to make them short and punchy, or just a single sentence. If it doesn't say how many words are expected, or what information is expected, it is very difficult to get work written correctly. The same goes for tasks or exercises which are set. If they aren't explained clearly, it is easy to not do the task or exercise at all, or not do it correctly. One way to look at things is 'what would someone who takes what is written down literally going to think they need to do based on how this is worded?', because that is how it is likely to get understood.

Sometimes what is needed is clarification, yet a student with Asperger's may not ask for clarification, so to find out whether they have correctly understood what they are to do needs more than just giving them a question and knowing they can read. It needs someone to talk with them and ask them what they plan to do to answer the question, or to carry out the task. You want to hear them tell you what you need to hear to let you know they have understood, and if it doesn't seem like they have understood, you can clarify things for them.

6. Learning-conducive environment

To work most efficiently the student will need an environment which is conducive to their way of learning. When it comes to things they are interested in, they may be able to focus or talk for hours without a break, but for other things, they may struggle to hold their focus, and to block out distractions.

An ideal environment is likely to be different for every student, and obviously a school can't cater for every student with their own personal environment, but they can find what suits many students with Asperger's.

Some things which often help are having lights which aren't too bright, or too dim. Dimmable lights are probably best, because then they can be altered through a range of brightnesses to suit different students. Fluorescent lighting often flickers violently and is terrible to have, and non-dimmable LED lights, although energy-efficient, can be painfully bright. Allowing students to do things which bring them comfort, as long as they aren't unhealthy or inappropriate coping mechanisms, is helpful. So, it could be that a student needs to wear sunglasses, headphones or a cap in the class to reduce sensory overload.

Create an environment which isn't busy, so give plenty of blank space where the student can look, or place them near a window if there is something like perhaps grass or trees or plants they can look at.

Allow the student to find where is comfortable for them to sit, rather than dictating where they sit. So, they may work better when they are tucked away in a corner, rather than in the middle of the room surrounded by students, creating surround-sound distraction.

Have low numbers of students in the class, where possible, and include students who are likely to have a calming influence on them, rather than students who are very active and perhaps have behavioural challenges which the student may copy, or become anxious.

Let the student doodle or do other things to occupy themselves while they listen to the lesson, and don't expect the student to try to make eye contact, because this can be an overwhelming experience. You just notice so much going on when you look closely at someone's face and eyes, and most students get overwhelmed with all of this information. They don't understand it, they just see it all.

7. Time

Giving the student extra time to do exams and projects will help them. Giving anyone more time is helpful, but for those with Asperger's, if they grasp what is expected of them - like having to write a report about something they are interested in - then they are likely to work quickly and efficiently and put in lots of hours to the work they are doing. But, if they have to work out what everything means, then this slows them right down, and can even make them grind to a halt.

When I was doing my GCSE exams, I took my Science exam and only completed about half of the paper, because I had to keep reading and rereading the questions to make sure I understood them. Being left-handed slowed me down some more, too, as I tried to write neatly without smudging my work. I got a Double C in my Science exam, and was told if I'd completed the paper I could get a Double A, or if I took the advanced paper I may even be able to get an A*. I didn't want to take the risk with the higher paper, because if I got lower than a C it was a fail, and I thought 'what if, on the day of the exam, I have an off day and my mind goes blank?' In the end, I did retake my Science exam, I still ran out of time and didn't complete the paper, but got a Double B. I also retook my English and Mathematics. With English Language and Maths, I finished more of my papers and improved my results, but in English Literature the extra time made no difference. I got an E the first time around and still got an E. I couldn't really grasp the questions. No amount of reading and rereading the questions helped me to understand what answers I was supposed to give. This wasn't so much a time issue; it was more an issue of struggling with concepts and getting into the writer's mind.

It may not always be possible to give students extra time, but where it is possible and where a teacher can't help with explaining and clarifying things – like in the middle of an exam – it is helpful.

Another element is the perception of time someone with Asperger's has. This can sometimes be very different to *real world time*. It is common, if they are thinking or focusing on something they are interested in, for hours to pass, and it will feel to them like just a couple of minutes have passed. This can cause a problem with time-keeping, where they may totally forget they are supposed to be somewhere, or they think a couple of minutes have passed, yet they have actually missed an appointment, or haven't arrived for a lesson... Or a lesson has ended and they have been so lost in thought they have barely started what they were supposed to be working on.

8. Helping the Asperger's student navigate school

Not all students with Asperger's are going to have issues with navigating school, but where they do, it is useful to find ways to help them. It could be giving them an easy to read map – nowadays this could probably even be an image on their mobile phone.

I am generally good at orienteering. I can read maps, and I don't usually get lost in the woods, yet, for some reason, in school I wouldn't be able to remember where one location was in relation to another. I could finish in an English lesson and need to get to a French lesson five minutes' walk away, and I wouldn't remember how to get there. Or a teacher would ask me to take something to a specific room somewhere in the school, as if somehow I knew what and where they were talking about. Really, I would have no idea. I would just be roaming around the school aimlessly until eventually something would click in my mind and I would realise where I was and where I needed to go. This still happens today. I can be in my local town centre and not know where I am and what direction I need to head to get to where my wife tells me she is. Or I can be on a local bus and not know where to get off because I don't recognise anything out of the windows. I don't know if I have passed my stop or not.

Another option can be to have someone navigate the school with the student, or - probably the preferred option for someone with Asperger's - to have all lessons in just one or two classrooms, and ideally with the same teacher, or just a small number of teachers. This option is obviously not feasible for mainstream school classrooms, but for independent educational establishments, and for some adult education courses and specialist schools, it may be a possible solution.

9. Student's interaction with others

The Asperger's student is likely to struggle with social interactions. They may avoid interactions. They may not want too many interactions. They may want the interactions, but not know how to have them, and so interact inappropriately.

Teachers can facilitate interactions, and help teach the student how it is appropriate to behave and interact with others. This should be being taught at home by the parents, but it is helpful if it is reinforced and also taught in school. It could be that the student has a class each week where they get to learn and practice social interaction, and strategies for managing emotions like anger and anxiety. Or, they could be observed in natural interactions, especially if they are younger children, and encouraged by the teacher to behave in specific ways and given real-time feedback about how they are doing socially. This can encourage them to stop doing the socially-inappropriate behaviours, and to do more of the socially-appropriate behaviours.

It can be helpful to pair them up with someone who is calm, patient and has good social skills, with whom they can interact during lessons, and hopefully form a friendship - although the student with Asperger's is likely to see friendships different to others, so they may well have a shallower view of what a friend is.

10. Discipline

Discipline needs to be timely. Giving a detention the next day is likely to be meaningless. It is better to give a small discipline immediately where appropriate. Like all students, the student should be treated fairly. Those with Asperger's often have a very strong view of fairness, and seldom lie. So if they feel that they are being treated unfairly – for example, if the whole class is being kept late because one or two of the children messed around, they are likely to see this as unfair, since they didn't do anything wrong. And, because they rarely lie, they are likely to tell the truth to people, even teachers. So when a teacher asks rhetorical questions, they may get an answer they didn't really ask for, and if the student feels they are being treated unfairly, they may well argue the case, and be very blunt about their opinions with their answers, because they don't necessarily have the social skills to answer in a more diplomatic way. They may also just talk with their actions and walk out of a room, not thinking of any consequences, because they haven't done anything wrong.

Unfortunately, this behaviour usually gets the student with Asperger's into further trouble, even though they will view the situation as them not doing anything wrong. To them, it is unfair to punish a whole classroom of children for the actions of a few.

Another thing to consider when disciplining a student with Asperger's is not to corner them, or to do things which could be seen as aggressive acts. Standing over the student when telling them off and talking assertively may well be seen as an act of aggression, to be fought or escaped; cornering a student near a wall, or other area where they don't have a clear path of escape, when telling them off may be seen as aggression. Their natural instinct in these moments will be to fight or run. If they are stopped from running – even if that is because the school is locked once pupils are inside – they will be in fight or flight mode. This part of the brain dims down the higher cortex, so they aren't likely to remember much about what happens, just a haze and a few flashes of memory, and probably the feelings. In this state, they may well do whatever they have to do to ensure their safety; they won't be thinking through the higher parts of their brain which would usually have them see harming people as wrong. If their only way to escape is to stab someone, or punch or kick or bite or headbutt, then they are very likely to just do it because they want to escape the situation.

If they can be kept calm, and if they aren't put in a position of feeling trapped, they are likely to think much more clearly and to make better decisions. The same applies if fellow students make them feel trapped. Because they struggle to understand facial expressions and emotions, they can react in ways which to them was the only way they could see in that moment to react, but to others, it may seem out of the blue, or over-the-top for the situation. If they have black-and-white thinking as well, this all-or-nothing thinking can contribute to the apparent over-reaction. So, it is best to be alongside them, not too close, and unthreatening – for example, down at their level, and not forcing eye contact, or forcing stopping their coping strategies, like doodling, tapping, or stimming, etc.

They should definitely have an easy way out if they want to take it. Just having a way out can often be enough to make the student feel comfortable that they don't need to escape, and so actually don't take the way out. It is generally best not to talk to someone about an incident for at least 24 hours, because even if they have psychologically calmed down they still have the stress hormones running through their body for many hours, and so it is easy for them to be re-provoked. And because memories are state-dependant the more angry and single minded they were at the time of the incident, the less likely they are to remember details or much about it when they are calm.

CHAPTER FOUR

Tips For Those With Asperger's

1. Relaxation

Relaxation is one of the most important skills someone can learn. High levels of emotion reduce the activity of the higher parts of the brain, so when someone is getting stressed, anxious or angry (or any other strong emotion), they will see the world rigidly; their ability to think flexibly will decrease, they will be more likely to see just one point of view, and it will increase the likelihood that they will make poor decisions.

For children and teens, when they are stressed, anxious or angry, they are likely to see just their perspective, believing that they are right. They are likely to see any challenge to this as a conflict which someone has to win; they are likely to fight to try to win if they are feeling angry, or to try to escape the conflict if they are feeling anxious.

In school, if people tried to give me the bumps, or tried to 'bundle' me for fun, I would suddenly feel a surge of anxiety. With the rapidly increasing anxiety I would quickly enter a fight-or-flight state of mind, where I would do whatever I had to do to prevent it from happening. My first instinct was to run, but I had no problem with the idea of trying to break fellow students' arms or legs, or trying to seriously hurt them in some other way. To me, in that state of mind, this was the only option I could see to ensure the thing which would cause me high levels of anxiety didn't happen. My mindset was to escape the threat first, or if that didn't work, to neutralise it.

There are many different ways you can relax, and there are a couple of different ways to look at relaxation. There are some techniques which can be done to be more relaxed generally, and some which you can do to relax when you are starting to feel emotions increasing.

General relaxation: Take a scale (say 1-10). If you have had a stressful day and are asked 'on a scale of 1-10, with 10 being most stressed, how stressed are you?' Say you answer that you are a 7/10. Then, anything else happening is very likely to tip you into unmanageable stress - just three points more and you will be at a 10/10. Whereas, if you have had the same stressful day, but you find a way to relax before carrying on with your evening, and you get yourself from a 7/10, down to 3/10, now the same three points only raise your stress levels to 6/10 - still less stressed than you felt before the evening.

This means you will be better able to handle situations, think clearly, and make better judgements and decisions.

Some techniques which work well for general relaxation include:

Meditation: Meditation takes two general forms, focused or mindful. With focused meditations, you are focusing in on one point and keeping your focus on that point, and if your attention strays, as soon as you recognise this you bring your attention back again. Mindfulness meditation is about being present, and not focusing specifically on any one thing. There is one warning in relation to mindfulness meditation which I don't often see mentioned, and that is that it can sometimes lead to people experiencing uncomfortable emotions. Traditionally, meditation wasn't about relaxation. Many people find it relaxing, but that isn't the purpose of it. With mindfulness meditation, the idea is to just observe ongoing experience. If that current experience is upsetting thoughts, or anxiety, or anger, then these thoughts can appear stronger because you aren't doing anything to distract yourself from them or to push them away. The idea is that you aren't attaching to the thoughts and feelings of your current ongoing experience, but if you are a beginner to mindfulness meditation, it is common to struggle to detach, and just accept that those ideas are there. With practice, you can get used to detaching yourself from the ongoing experience, and when you are detached, you enter a relaxed mind-body state because you aren't connecting with any emotions. As you develop this skill, not only will you find general levels of relaxation increasing, but you will be able to handle emotionally arousing situations better as well.

There isn't a secret formula to meditation. It is easier to do in a quiet dimly-lit place, and with your eyes closed, but this isn't essential, and it is useful if you practice using it in everyday life. So, if you are walking along, rather than talking to yourself, pay attention to many different things and practice meditative walking. As you are walking along, either focus on the walking, or just walk along being mindful - not specifically focusing on the walking, but not talking to yourself and letting any thoughts which happen to spontaneously arise drift into consciousness and back away again without addressing them or doing anything with them. This state of mind is often described as a flow-state. It is common for sports players to describe being in the zone, where they are just aware - not thinking about what they needed to do, or any other thoughts or ideas, they were just in the moment, reacting to the moment. This is when people often perform most optimally. Doing meditation like this and making it a part of everyday life and routine has huge benefits, it can be challenging to begin with, but, like anything else, it gets easier with practice. Another way you can meditate to relax is to use guided meditation. This can be done by just closing your eyes and imagining something. But it is easier if the guided meditation is audio recorded, so that you can listen along. This helps to prevent having to focus on what you are supposed to do.

Unlike meditation as described above, guided meditations can be done specifically to help you to relax. They usually take the form of a journey, or they have transitions of some sort. Journeys and transitions deepen the experience. People prefer different things, and there is a lot of variety, so if one thing doesn't work for you, that doesn't mean something else won't work instead. Some people respond well to pretty much any guided meditation; others like it 'just right'. For example; I prefer guided meditations spoken by a deep male voice. I like meditations with sound effects – the sound of being on a beach, if it is a beach meditation, I like meditations which are slow with plenty of silence (which also deepens the state), but someone else may prefer meditations by women, or they may not like sound effects or music in the meditation, and they may prefer something which is faster-paced. It is about trying a variety of different meditations and finding out what you like. You can also record your own.

Some meditations focus on journeys or transitions like walking along a beach, or through the woods, or travelling down a river through a jungle. Or, a transition could be something like walking through an art gallery and stepping into a painting, or walking through the woods and finding and entering a hut, or walking through the arctic and entering an igloo. Another approach is for the journey to be through your body. Generally, meditations involving your body can be good for helping with relaxation. This type of approach is commonly called progressive muscle relaxation. There are different ways you can do this, and as with other guided meditation, you can either guide yourself, or use an audio recording. Again, you will want to find a recording which has the pace and approach suited to you.

I personally prefer the focus to be from the top down, as to me, this implies going deeper, and relaxing more, whereas going from the feet up feels like it is the wrong way round. So, as I talk about it here, I will talk about the head down, rather than feet up. One approach is to focus on each part of your body in turn, and then with a relaxing deep outbreath you let your focus move down to the next part of your body. So you focus on the top of your head, taking a deep breath in, then pause a moment, then give a deep breath out and let the focus move down to your face, and repeat this all the way down to your toes. Another approach can be to tense up each body part as you focus on it, this is good if you already have some tension there, so you focus on the top of your head, scrunch up your forehead, and face, etc., hold that tension for a few seconds, then let that tension go, and let your focus of attention move to your neck, and keep repeating this all the way down through your body.

You can imagine a light passing through your body from the top of your head down, with each part of your body relaxing as the light passes through that part of the body. This could be a white light, or different coloured light, or if you wanted to it could be focusing on light passing through the chakras of your body, with the light changing and a sense of it cleansing your body as it goes.

Relaxing hobbies and interests: If there is something you do which helps you to relax, then this could be it for you. So, if you find running or exercising relaxes you, then you can make more time to do this. If listening to certain music helps to relax you, then you can find time to listen to this, and make it a time you can focus on just listening to the music, where you won't be disturbed by other things. If it is reading, then you can find time when you won't be disturbed and just focus on reading.

Self-hypnosis: Something else you can do to relax is self-hypnosis. Self-hypnosis is very similar to meditation. The main difference is that meditation traditionally isn't directive. There isn't a goal, as such; it is more about experience. Self-hypnosis, on the other hand, is usually directive - you do it for a purpose or goal. With self-hypnosis you can either do it to yourself, or, like with the meditation, you can follow along to someone guiding you through the experience. If you are doing it for yourself, then you can either follow a structured approach, like that where you begin focusing on a spot on a wall and noticing three things you can see, three things you can hear, and three things you can feel, then repeating this with your eyes closed, then opening your eyes again and noticing two things you can see, two things you can hear, and two things you can feel, then closing your eyes and repeating this, then opening your eyes and noticing one thing you can see, one thing you can hear, and one thing you can feel, then closing your eyes and repeating this. Once you have done this, you could let your focus drift to what you hope to achieve, so it could be just to relax and enjoy to relaxation, perhaps tell yourself you would like to learn how to be more relaxed in stressful situations. Then after about 15 minutes, you are likely to just drift out of the experience and open your eyes.

There are other self-hypnosis techniques you can use which are equally easy to do. Alternatively, you can listen to a guided self-hypnosis audio recording. Like with meditation, this has the advantage of allowing the listener to focus on just relaxing, rather than having to have a part of themselves trying to focus on the process, and on what they need to do. A guided self-hypnosis audio recording is also likely to be able to guide you through mentally rehearsing different situations which make you feel stressed; there are also likely to be post-hypnotic suggestions for responding differently in the future. Post-hypnotic suggestions are ideas given during hypnosis to influence behaviour after the hypnosis has ended, so there could be a suggestion that in the future, when you enter a specific situation you will feel calm and relaxed, and this suggestion will increase the chances of responding in that way in those situations. Like meditation, self-hypnosis isn't a quick fix. You are likely to need to listen to a self-hypnosis recording, or use self-hypnosis often, before you notice the benefits. The process of being hypnotised is likely to be a relaxing experience, and in my private practice I find that if someone is hypnotised, they exit hypnosis feeling very relaxed and calm.

Even without suggestions for carrying on feeling relaxed, they feel far more relaxed for the rest of the day, and often into the next day, and often report that they sleep really well that night. Therapeutic change, though, often requires some time, and real-life changes, not just a change of mind, so the listener may well need to change their behaviour as well.

Relaxing in the moment: There are a number of different ways to relax in the moment depending on the circumstances.

7-11 breathing: 7-11 breathing is where you breathe in counting to seven, pause for a moment, and then breathe out counting to eleven. Breathing in activates the sympathetic nervous system – the stress response – and breathing out activates the parasympathetic nervous system – the relaxation response. With 7-11 breathing you are extending the out-breath, which encourages relaxation. In normal, everyday life, your in-breath and out-breath are about even, when you panic the in-breath is longer than the out-breath. If you check your pulse as you breathe slowly you can notice the change to your pulse while you breathe, and notice that, as you take a long breath in, your heart rate increases, and as you then take a long breath out your heart rate slows down.

7-11 breathing can be done anywhere, anytime. It is one of my favourite techniques because it can be done without anyone noticing too. I remember working with a family where the daughter had 'anger problems', according to the school and the parent. The school sent her to their in-house anger management programme for teens; they taught her to clench one of her fists when she was feeling stressed or angry, to hold her fist clenched for a few moments, before relaxing the fist and letting the tension go. Unfortunately, this wasn't the best advice; it didn't help her relax, and the other more significant issue was that she had a reputation for hitting other students when they made her angry, so when they were making her angry and they saw her clench her fist, they thought she was about to hit them! I taught her 7-11 breathing as a way she could relax without it being obvious to other students that she was doing a technique, and without anyone misinterpreting her behaviour, this had a huge impact on how she got on in school, and at home with siblings and with her mum.

Sitting down: Another way to relax yourself is to sit down, if it is safe and possible to do so. When I used to work in residential homes with children and teens who were often very aggressive and violent, sitting down was one of my main tactics for managing their aggression. If I felt sitting would put me at risk of harm, I wouldn't use this technique, but if the child or teen was just shouting aggressively and I didn't feel that they were likely to physically attack me, then I would sit.

There are certain actions which increase anger in yourself and others. When we are angry we want to make ourselves as big and as intimidating as we can. Often, if someone is sitting down and they become angry, they jump up out of their seat, they get very close, and they broaden their chest, often spreading their arms to make themselves as large as possible.

When you feel yourself getting angry or anxious, it is helpful to take control of what you can about your behaviour. Your physical behaviour is one of those things you can control. When you sit down you may be feeling angry, anxious or scared, and you may want to stand, but by controlling yourself and remaining seated you will start to calm down as, physically, your body language isn't the body language of an angry, anxious or scared person. It is also good to talk with a calm and soft voice. Again, your voice is something you can control, so if you are talking calmly and in a relaxed manner, this too will help you to relax.

If you are in a situation which makes you feel anxious or angry, then sitting down is helpful. For example, I find giving talks about a subject I'm not familiar with can make me anxious, so if I have the opportunity, I will do the talk sitting down. Sometimes I've had to do talks where I can't sit down fully, because I will be too low, so I may turn a chair around and "perch" on the back of the chair, so although I am pretty much standing, I feel like I am sitting. This then means I can relax my muscles to some extent, as the chair takes my weight. I always relax my shoulders as well. This is another great way to create relaxation and reduce anger or anxiety; just relax your arms and shoulders, and breathe deeply and calmly, and after a while this starts to happen automatically.

Focusing internally: Another useful strategy for relaxing in the moment is to learn to focus internally. This is a strategy I use mainly when I'm out in busy locations, or on public transport. If I have headphones - ideally noise-cancelling headphones - then I will use these to help me shut out some of the stimulus. Sunglasses can also help, not just with light, but with dimming down all the movement. Sometimes I will wear noise-cancelling headphones with nothing playing through them, just to reduce the noise of the outside world. Other times, though, it is useful to have something playing. I have a playlist on my mp3 player of relaxing music, largely with no singing, so it makes good background music which I won't get distracted by. If there are lyrics to the songs it is easy to find myself singing along in my head to the tune, which becomes a distraction from whatever I'm actually trying to spend my time doing. I also have tracks which are just natural sounds, like sounds of woodland, birds, whales, the ocean, or other relaxing environments.

Wearing headphones and sunglasses can help to reduce the outside world, which helps me to be able to focus internally. And when I focus internally, I can become very unresponsive externally, so if someone tries to get my attention, I may end up ignoring them. This is absolutely not because I am rude, but because I am largely unaware of them. So, if you are going to use strategies like this which can make you less responsive to others, then it is useful to mention to friends, family, loved ones or others you who may try talking to you that you are going to relax, and so you may be less responsive - that you aren't being rude and ignoring them!

To focus internally, I defocus my eyes a little and focus on my breathing, and on other things I'm doing in the moment. If I'm walking around, this is about as much as I would usually do, because I still need to be able to navigate the world around me, so I can't be totally shut off from reality. If I am sitting down, in a café, for example, or on a bus or train (I will do this even if I'm standing on public transport), then I will let myself get drawn into my mind. I will think of things I like. For me, I am often in my mind making plans for things, or working through different invention ideas and how they would work, or different scientific theories which haven't been proved correct but which may be correct. I may be thinking about what impact different ideas would have on the world if they were correct, or I imagine doing hypnosis with different hypothetical people, considering what I would observe about them, and what those observations would teach me about the person, and how I would respond to the person based on my observations. I let myself get fully absorbed in this inner world, and after a short while, even when my eyes are open, I stop noticing things in the real world, because all I am focusing on is the world inside my mind. By focusing on these things internally, I'm not focusing on anxiety or anger, or on environmental anxiety or anger triggers, so my body becomes relaxed as I am busy in my mind.

Reading and other engaging activities: Reading a book is another good way to relax in the moment. If you are focused on reading, then you stop focusing on everything outside of the book. This is also true if you are focused perhaps on playing a handheld games console, or a game on a mobile phone, tablet or laptop, or if you are listening to an audiobook. If you allow your attention to be drawn into that engaging activity, then you stop focusing on any anxiety or anger thoughts, and because you aren't focusing on these thoughts, your body and mind relax.

2. Learn social communication skills

One thing which transformed my life was discovering hypnosis as a teenager. Hypnosis is all about communication skills. On the surface, it looks like hypnotists somehow magically tell people what to do and people comply. When I first started learning about hypnosis I thought it was all about the scripts hypnotists used, and I thought you had to find the right wording to make people do what you want, but the reality of hypnosis is somewhat different.

The communication skills I learned from studying hypnosis as a teenager weren't taught in school, or by parents, or anyone else. Hypnosis talks about eye contact, about personal space, and gestures, and breathing patterns - all things which are useful to learn.

Some tips for things to learn as a teen or child are to understand eye contact. In hypnosis, there is something taught called the *hypnotic gaze*. This is a way to look at someone, seeming to make eye contact with them, and using this eye contact to help induce hypnosis. How it works, in reality though, is that you either look through the person, so although you are looking in line with their eyes, you are actually looking at a point behind the person, or you look at the bridge of the person's nose. This gives them the feeling that you are looking directly into both of their eyes. Eye contact isn't all or nothing. People generally make eye contact while they are talking to someone, then every time they think about something - perhaps what they will say next - they break eye contact to think, then make eye contact again. The listener generally makes eye contact as they are being talked to, and anytime they think about something - perhaps about how they will reply to the person talking - they break eye contact, before making eye contact again. The eye contact isn't constant. Although the person probably feels like they were making eye contact, their eyes are actually looking around the other person's face, mainly focusing on the eyes and mouth, but also covering the rest of the face, because they are reading the communication of the person to get a fuller idea of what is being communicated. For example, when the person smiles as they hear what they are being told do, they show signs of it being a genuine smile. As they are being told something which the speaker thinks could be embarrassing to say, does the listener show a facial expression of disgust as they smile and nod politely? Or do they show anger, or another emotion? Unconsciously, they are looking at various other parts of the person's face to gather this communication, as well as the spoken part of it.

When I was a teen I didn't know as much detail about all of this as I do now, so I used to use the hypnotic gaze, and made eye contact while counting in my mind to five, then I'd break eye contact counting to five, and repeat this pattern. This was a simplistic solution, but it helped me to fit better with how everyone else was communicating.

Learning about personal space is important, too. People all have a space they don't like strangers entering - usually over a couple of metres; they have a space which friends can enter - usually just over a metre; and they have a space which those close to them can enter - usually less than a metre. As someone with Asperger's, I usually prefer to keep away from people generally and not have people hug me, or make close contact with me. It may seem odd mentioning this, because you may think you aren't likely to have a problem with getting too close to someone, but sometimes other thoughts take over. So, if you have to go and talk to someone, it is easy to just walk up to the person and stand wherever you end up and talk to them, even if this is right next to them. Or, you may see something you like on them - it could be a book they are holding, or the texture of an item of clothing - and so you grab at it without thinking about that being too personal.

One challenge can be how you define 'friend'. For me, I either don't know someone at all, or I know them - in which case, I would say that is a friend according to how my mind works. Alternatively, you are in a relationship with them, in which case they are close; yet, I know my wife doesn't think of everyone she knows as being a friend. She has more variety, she has people she knows who are acquaintances, people whom she may say are just work colleagues, people she doesn't particularly like, people whom she would say are close friends. She has many layers which I don't have. I treat all people who aren't my wife as she would treat acquaintances, whether they are family, what she would say are my friends, or my acquaintances, or work colleagues. So, I try to take my lead from how each treats me when they meet me. I try to let them define how close they will get to me, and whatever they set I don't get closer than this. It is helpful to take your lead from others, I will never instigate hugging or kissing when greeting or saying goodbye, but will accept it if they do it to me. I let others define the situation, as long as it doesn't cause me anxiety beyond what I am comfortable managing. So I don't like being hugged, but it is a brief moment of discomfort, not prolonged, and it isn't a socially unacceptable or inappropriate behaviour they are doing. If it was, I wouldn't accept it.

Another social communication skill is to use empathetic statements or questions (depending on how you say it). So, when someone is complaining about something that happened, you can reply with "sounds like it was a really difficult situation". You may not care about what the person has said, but this type of comment makes people feel listened to and empathised with. If you say that sentence with an upward inflection with your voice at the end of the sentence, it will come across like a question and the person will carry on talking about the situation, taking it as you wanting to know more. Likewise, if you say the sentence with a downward inflection at the end, it will come across like a statement, and the common response is for them to feel heard - like their feelings about the situation have been acknowledged.

It is important to find a way which works for you to learn communication skills, to learn what different facial expressions mean. Check out the work of Dr Paul Ekman for some helpful information about this, and study social psychology and body language books - although don't take things rigidly. I went for a job interview a couple of months after I was run over. I was interviewed by a panel. I got the job, but due to my injuries I couldn't stay in the job. I saw the company's interview notes. I knew they were trained in neuro-linguistic programming before I went for the interview, but I didn't realise how rigidly they stuck to what they were taught. They wrote that I wasn't very open, and appeared to be trying to hide something during the interview because I kept crossing my arms. The reality was that I had an injured right arm, and the chair I was on didn't have armrests, so I kept having to put my arm on my lap and hold it in place with my left hand. I wasn't hiding anything.

Studying body language is helpful, but the most important thing to remember is that you are looking for patterns in behaviour, not just an isolated example of a behaviour. If someone crosses their arms every time a specific thing is mentioned, then it may be relevant, but you have to start from a place of not knowing and coming up with all the different meanings you can think of for what you are observing. So, crossing arms could be because they have an injury, or it could be because it is more comfortable for them, or because they are cold, or because they are uncomfortable talking about something.

I was fortunate that I have spent much of my life obsessed with hypnosis and related topics. Even if you aren't obsessed with this, it is still definitely worth learning as much as you can about things related to people, including psychology, social science, body language, language and metaphor use, how different cultures view the world, and differences in people based on where they spent most of their childhood. Those who grow up in dense cities usually have closer personal space, than those who grow up in sparse villages, for example. I worked somewhere where people felt uncomfortable with one of the members of staff, as he would stand almost nose-to-nose when talking to people. He grew up in a densely-populated location and, to him, close proximity to others was normal. Yet, to most people in the workplace, his level of proximity made them feel uncomfortable and threatened. He needed to learn that his behaviour made others uncomfortable, and that he needed to work at giving people space; at the same time, others needed to understand he wasn't trying to be threatening.

Another important skill I practiced when I was a teenager was how to smile. It is difficult to explain, but to make the muscles around the eyes move so that the smile appears genuine, you have to practice tensing the muscles around the side towards the back of the head, so that you pull your ears back, then lift the muscles around the side of the face, narrow the eyes as you pull the muscles around the outside edge of the eyes up and back, and then smile with your mouth.

3. Find a friend

When I was in primary school, I learned that if I had a friend, that person could be a conduit between myself and the rest of the world. I had someone who could do the things I wasn't comfortable doing, while I did things they didn't like doing. So I would do tedious tasks which they didn't like doing, and they would go and ask teachers for things, and do social things.

Obviously, as an adult, I don't think it is right to have friend, because they can do things which I can't do, but having a friend is certainly helpful. Even as an adult, if I have a friend who can introduce me to people, and who can start conversations, this helps tremendously, as does having someone who can make phone calls on my behalf. I am honest with friends about needing their help, and not being good at these things, but as a child it didn't cross my mind to tell them I'm not good at some things (which is why I'm getting them to do those things), but I'm more comfortable doing other things (which is why I'm offering to do those things in return).

Finding a friend will help to improve your communication skills as you practice communicating with them, too. It is naturally good when the two of you have plenty of different skills so that you complement each other. You will also learn about having to put in effort to maintain the friendship, which is a valuable skill for the future, because if you don't bother to keep in contact with the friend, and you don't give anything to the friendship - you just take, and you don't show interest in them, or in things they are interested in - then they will stop wanting to spend time with you.

4. Space

Finding ways to have your own space, and making others aware of where you go is important. As a child and young teenager, I used to go into the woods; as an older teenager I had moved to a seaside town, so I used to go to sit on a quiet beach; and as an adult I used to sit on the beach if I wanted to get out of home. At home, sometimes I would make a tent on the sofa by draping a blanket over the back of the sofa and having it hang down the front. Sometimes, my wife will make me a den under the dining room table for me to go into, or I will sit in the bathroom in the dark and quiet so that there isn't any sensory input. In school and workplaces, it is useful to negotiate a space you can go when you need to, and create your space how you want it for you. For example, for me, I needed my workspace to be clear of distractions, so I didn't put anything on my desk dividers. I just kept the plain blue so that I could stare into this when I needed to focus and shut everything else out.

5. Nature

From those I have spoken to, nature is very important and calming. Many with Asperger's seem to have an affinity with animals, wildlife and being in nature. If you live in a city or don't have access to wildlife, or proper nature, but find it helps you, it is useful to have substitutes. I have natural sounds on my Walkman that I listen to, then with my eyes closed, I could easily be sitting listening to those natural sounds for real. I still know I'm not, but I prefer it to listening to music or the real-world environment. I will also have photographs and videos which I will watch, and even computer games I play, to give me a sense of being in nature when I don't have the opportunity. I will play games like the Elder Scrolls games, and just walk around the environments, relaxing, or stopping by a river, or watching a sunset in-game.

6. Understand others don't think or feel the same way

It always shocks me that others don't think or feel the same as me. I logically know it, but I still get surprised. For example, a few years ago, a DVD documentary about Milton Erickson was released. Because it was a documentary about Milton Erickson, I assumed millions of people around the world would be buying it, so I woke up early on the day of release and kept refreshing the website webpage, waiting for it to say the DVD was available to order, and I ordered it as soon as the button said I could. I was worried that if I didn't buy it straight away it would sell out and I would miss out. My wife told me that most people don't know who Milton Erickson is, and wouldn't be trying to buy the DVD. She was probably correct, but I only realise that when I logically and rationally analyse my behaviour. I don't know why millions of people wouldn't want the DVD, but I do understand, most of the time, that not everyone thinks the same.

It is important to realise this and to try to get into the mindset of others, try to think what might they be thinking. I will sit in cafés and public places watching people. I will try to get into their mindset, and work out what they might be thinking and what behaviour makes me think that, and what behaviour I expect to see next. I try to learn what people think about situations, and listen to what people say about things, and whether I agree with them or not. I have a general rule, that if someone thinks differently to me, the most likely possibility is that most people think like that other person rather than me.

An example of this is relationships ending. When I had a long-term relationship end my best friend believed I should go out drinking. I should have been angry with the person, I should have wanted to emotionally hurt her, I shouldn't want to be nice to her, I should have wanted to grieve the loss of the relationship. The more I told him that wasn't me, the more he told me that meant I was in denial. I didn't want to go out drinking, I didn't feel a need to. I didn't feel angry. I had no negative feelings towards the person, and I had moved on and was just carrying on with my life. What I learned was that he probably viewed relationship break-ups like that, and that is probably how most people view relationships break-ups.

7. Tackling bullying and discrimination

Bullying and discrimination is common among those on the autistic spectrum. If you don't have a diagnosis, but would be very likely to get a diagnosis if you went for an assessment, then it can sometimes be helpful to have that diagnosis. This helps you to access occupational health support, and to be able to take action against discrimination for having a disability. It is helpful to talk to people about bullying or discrimination and to ask for help, but what bullying or discrimination is happening will decide who you may talk to. It could be a parent, the HR department in your work, or the citizens' advice bureau. For managing bullying, learning to be assertive is helpful. This is different to aggression; assertiveness is stating what you want to say clearly and calmly, and sticking to what you are saying, not getting drawn into arguments or discussions, just stating facts. As well as learning assertiveness skills, it is important where possible not to react with aggression, or an emotion which makes the bully feel they have got to you. Most bullies want a reaction, so if you give them a reaction, they may like it, and so keep bullying.

When I was in secondary school, some teens tried to bully me. They called me names, and pushed me to the ground. I stood up and carried on walking. They pushed me to the ground again. I stood up and carried on walking. They did the same again, as did I, and then they left me alone. I was no fun to bully. I wasn't intimidated and I didn't get angry.

8. Asking for help, and keeping people informed

Asking for help can be difficult when you don't think about it. I know this is often my problem. Asking for help is an important skill to learn. It could be that you need help to understand something in school or college, or help to understand something in work, or in a job application. Sometimes, people are so confident in the instructions they have given that you assume you must know what something means, when in reality you are just doing what you *think* you are supposed to be doing. People generally don't mind if you ask for help, and if you ask for clarity about things, like the way something is worded, asking for help also makes people like you more because they helped you. I had my end-of-year appraisal to write up one year. I spent hours working on what I was writing, writing what I thought the answers should be, based on what I thought the questions were. When I went into my meeting with my manager to talk through my appraisal, they told me off for clearly showing no regard for the appraisal process, clearly not putting any time into what I had written. To them, obviously didn't take it seriously. I wasn't expecting to get told off; actually, I thought I had done a good job with my appraisal. It definitely wasn't a positive experience. My mistake was not asking for help a month earlier, when I'd started filling in my appraisal. I should have asked for clarity about all the questions before making a start, just to make sure I'd done it correctly. Had I done that, just to make sure I definitely understood everything, that meeting would have probably gone very differently.

Keeping people informed is another area to develop, especially when you are in work. It is all too easy to work on something, and once it is completed, move on to the next thing, and go through everything in a logical way. I like lists, so I will do this with lists. I will do the first thing, tick it off, then do the second thing and tick it off, and keep working down my list. What I forget to do is to tell my manager what I have completed. So, they could expect something completed within a week. I've completed it within a couple of days, and moved on to the next thing, and three weeks later they are asking me if I've completed the job they told me to do. I tell them I have, and give it to them; instead of them being pleased, they are annoyed that I hadn't told them it was done. It can be really difficult to approach people and talk with them - one of the reasons I wouldn't do it was that I didn't know which specific things I should tell them… Should I tell them every time I complete anything they ask me to do, or only specific things? It is their responsibility to let me know when they want me to feed things back to them; but it is your responsibility to make sure they know they need to tell you.

Another example is when I was a middle manager, a member of my staff had an accident and went to hospital. It wasn't a work accident, but it meant they had to go off sick. I was their direct line manager so I filled out the relevant forms, submitted them to HR, remained in contact with the member of staff for updates when necessary, and did everything I was supposed to do for my role, except I didn't tell my manager that a member of my staff was off sick due to an injury. I just carried on with everything else I had to do. I didn't think that they would need to know, but obviously, once this happened, I didn't make the same mistake again. So it is important to explain the way you think about things, and the way you do things, and what your strengths and weaknesses are, and to establish expectations, whether this is in an educational, work-based, or any other setting.

9. Dating and relationship skills

You will have advanced well with dating and relationship skills if you have been learning communication skills. There are, however, some extra bits which are important to know are around dating, and around keeping a relationship going.

Relationships can be tough, because you have to dedicate time to think about and consider the other person, not just focusing on yourself and your own interests. It is good to end up in relationships with people who understand you and your traits, and who fit with those traits. So a partner who is very needy may demand too much of you when you want your own space, and you don't want too much touching, for example. A partner who expects you to make all the decisions if you aren't good at making certain types of decisions (because perhaps you worry about making the wrong type of decision, or doing the wrong thing) may not be helpful, for example. It is best to be yourself, and to be open and honest. The right person will like you for who you are. This is better than being liked for who you were when you first met!

Dating is generally straightforward. I remember in school, as a teen, there was a girl I had asked out for nearly everyone I knew. I decided one day that I actually wanted to go out with her, and thought to myself, given that, why haven't I asked her out for *me*? I thought about what I would say and her possible answers – yes or no, or some version of these. I could think of what I could do if she said yes, but I couldn't think of what I was supposed to say if she said no; thus, I spoke to her just before the end of the lunch break, so that the bell would go and I would have to dash off. I thought this would be a good way around dealing with her saying no. When I asked her out, she said yes, and I regretted leaving it until the bell was about to go, as I had to arrange to meet up and then dash off.

When you ask people out that you like there are only two classes of answer you will get – yes or no. The answer may come in a variety of different words, but it will still be yes, or it will be no. If they don't want to go out with you, that is fine - it just means they weren't the right person for you anyway. You can just say 'okay' and walk away. If they say yes, then you can acknowledge this and follow it up with something, perhaps asking what they are interested in, and starting a conversation about this, and keep as much focus on them and on making them feel interesting.

As an adult, you rarely just ask someone out, you want to keep it natural with the environment you are in. So, if you are in a club or bar, or café, perhaps you could ask them if you can buy them a drink. If they say no, you can easily say 'cool' or 'okay' and walk away. If they say yes, then strike up a conversation like above. I remember hearing advice once, that all you need to do with dating is to walk up to someone and say, "Hi, I'm Dan" (or whatever your name is), and if they respond with their name, then continue the conversation; if they brush you off, then move on.

If you don't feel you come across well when you talk to people, you can learn how to act confident. True confidence only comes from knowing you can do something, but even before you know you can do something, you can appear confident. You can also learn how to talk with a calm and confident, friendly-sounding voice, remembering to smile as you talk, and using your communication skills, like eye contact.

To maintain a relationship, whether it is with a partner or with friends, you need to show interest in them, and make them feel interesting. Have the focus of conversations on them and not yourself, tell them about yourself and about traits you have which are useful for them to know. Open up conversation about things like contacting each other, so that you can establish expectations, and so that they don't think you don't like them just because you haven't thought to contact them for six months, and that they may need to think about contacting you, as you won't remember to contact them - remember to establish how often, too.

10. Seeking diagnosis

When seeking a diagnosis, you will need make an appointment with your GP. In the appointment, you will need to say what behaviours and traits you have that make you think you may have autism. You will have to say why it is you want the diagnosis; you are only likely to get a diagnosis if you can demonstrate that you are affected by having autism, and where a diagnosis would be helpful. It could be that you want the diagnosis to be able to access occupational health support, or to be able to tackle discrimination you are experiencing. You will need to explain how your behaviour and traits happen in all areas of your life, and how you have been like this all of your life.

All of this information needs to be on the letter the GP sends to the team which does diagnoses in your area. If the letter doesn't contain supporting information to make them think you may be on the autistic spectrum, they will reject the letter.

The assessment, then, will usually consist of some detailed questionnaires to fill out that will be sent to you in advance, you may be asked to post these back a couple of weeks before the face-to-face assessment, or you may be asked to bring them to the assessment. You will be probably be asked to bring a parent or someone with a similar role along to the assessment with you, as they will need to talk to this person about your early childhood and what you were like. Sometimes they will accept talking to the parent on the phone, but often when this happens, they still want to meet the parent face-to-face. If there are reasons why this can't happen, then you will have to talk with the assessor about what you should do instead. Usually, you will be told the outcome of your assessment at the end of the assessment, and will have to wait a few weeks for the report to be written confirming your diagnosis. Asperger's isn't a diagnosis now; it is just at the high-functioning end of autism spectrum disorder.

Dan Jones

CHAPTER FIVE

Additional Tips For Adults With Asperger's

1. Restaurants and shopping tips

Something which many with Asperger's find challenging is interacting with staff in restaurants and shops. I often have my wife around to do the interacting, so one option which can help is if you are somewhere with a friend or partner, they could talk to staff for you. For example, if my wife and I go out for the day, and decide we are going to get a Burger King or something for lunch, then I will usually have my wife get the food while I find the table. In shops, I will have my wife talk to staff if I need a refund or have a question, and in restaurants, my wife will often ask for the bill.

This isn't always a suitable option, though, so although it may be uncomfortable, sometimes we have to do things ourselves. For asking for food, for example, it is useful to keep a prompt - have a menu with you so that you can keep referring to it, especially if the staff keep asking you to repeat things. In shops, plan what you need to say. If you can do something with someone else first, this helps you to learn the process for when you are going to have to do it yourself. You can then practice this process in your mind. In restaurants, it can be challenging to get attention; saying "excuse me" while smiling slightly and talking calmly is probably the best option. The hardest part is trying to get attention without appearing rude, and in restaurants, also accepting that the staff will keep coming over and asking if everything is okay. You can use relaxation techniques to manage this if you find it annoying. If shops or venues are too much sensory overload, make sure anyone you are with knows what your plan is. For example, if out with my wife, I tell her that if it gets too much for me I will wait outside on a bench, or I will go and sit in a café. You can use noise-cancelling headphones and sunglasses to reduce visual and auditory sensory input, but unfortunately there isn't much you can do to reduce overcrowding and being bumped into all the time - all you can do is try to go to places which are quiet. In restaurants, you can ask for a table you would feel most comfortable at (which, in my case, is often in a corner); if it is busy, I prefer to be facing the wall or looking out of a window over a quiet view.

2. Public transport

Frequently, public transport is overcrowded. It can be noisy and a real attack on the senses. Sunglasses and noise-cancelling headphones can help, as can using relaxation techniques or listening to something relaxing. One challenge on public transport can be the uncertainty: not knowing when it is time to get off the bus or train, or not recognising where you are. Relaxation techniques, like 7-11 breathing, can help with this uncertainty, because they will help bring down anxiety levels. On many buses, you can also ask the driver to let you know when you are approaching your destination, and then sit near the driver, or use a map app on your mobile to track the journey. If possible, you can make new journeys with someone else first so that you have an idea of where you need to go, key landmarks on that journey, and landmarks approaching your destination.

Dan Jones

CHAPTER SIX

Interview Tips For Those With Asperger's

1. Relaxation

It is important to be relaxed in interviews. Many people with Asperger's seem to struggle with interviews, and get anxious about them. Really, interviews are structured and have a process, so there is no need to be anxious. Even though you want to be relaxed, and so can use relaxation techniques before (and during) the interview, you also want to appear keen and slightly nervous that you may not get the job, even if you aren't really nervous. I went for an interview once, and it was a group interview. I didn't get the job, so I asked why. I was told I was too relaxed and so obviously didn't want it. The reason I was relaxed was that I knew the job very well, and knew the answer to anything they could possibly ask me about the job. I wasn't anxious about not knowing anything, or about whether I would be offered the job, because that was out of my control. So you may have to come across like you really want the job, and are perhaps nervous they might not offer it to you.

2. Structure

Interviews have a clear structure. If it is a single interviewer, they are likely to have a list of questions they will ask you, mostly asking you to give evidence that you are likely to be able to do the job, and perhaps some questions to try to judge the type of person you are. If it is a panel interview, then each panel member will be likely to have set questions they will ask you. They will probably ask you either one question each, and then go back to the first person and ask their second question each, and repeat this, or they will have one person asking all of their questions, then the next person will ask all of their questions, etc. If it is a group interview you may be observed interacting with others who are also being assessed, to look for a suitable candidate. The idea isn't necessarily to take control of the situation, or to be the most dominant person, but to demonstrate that you are right for the role you are applying for. They are likely to also be judging how you behave towards others in the room.

After the questions, you normally get asked if you have any questions. This is always a good time to clarify what will happen next - like when will you find out the results of the interview - and anything else you feel you need to know, and then you will be dismissed. Prior to the interview, too, you can usually get in touch with the contact person on the job interview invite letter and explain you have autism spectrum disorder, stating that it would be helpful if you could know the structure of the interview. Some places will tell you this already in the letter, but you can often get more details by contacting the company.

3. Eye contact, looking at each interviewer

During the interview, you want to make eye contact with the person or people doing the interview. If it is a panel interview, you want to make eye contact with the person who just asked you the question first, then as you are answering make eye contact with the others on the panel too. As you do this, it is helpful to nod slightly while you are answering the question, because this encourages agreement from the interviewers. Then, as you finish answering the question you want to be looking back at the person who asked you the question. You want to look at the person asking the question slightly more than the others on the panel.

4. Smiling

In the interview, you want to appear friendly and kind, and likeable. Smiling encourages people to think this of you, so as you answer questions you want to talk with a smile; this also adds some character to your voice.

5. Thinking time

There is nothing wrong with pausing to think on how you are about to answer a question. It is better to give yourself a few moments' thinking time, than to rush out an answer and, halfway through talking, to think of what you should have been saying. If you have said you have Asperger's beforehand, and even in the interview explained that sometimes you just need a moment to think about your answer before you give it, they will appreciate this and, because they are letting you have thinking time and you have asked them to allow this, they will actually like you more; people like people more when they do something for the person.

6. Asking for the question to be clarified/asking for an example of the type of answer they are looking for

Many people think they will come across as stupid if they ask for a question to be clarified, or for an example of the type of answer the interviewer is looking for, but the reality is that it shows great strength of character. An employer is going to prefer someone who clarifies things and then does it right, rather than someone who is too nervous to ask and does something wrong. You will give better answers if you ask for clarity, and you can pretty much give an answer just like the example they give you, which is what they have said they want. Also, as mentioned in the section on thinking time, because they have helped you, they will like you more – commonly known as the Benjamin Franklin effect.

7. Preparation

It is important to prepare for every interview. You want to know details about the company you are applying to work for, about the role you will be doing, what skills and traits you need to demonstrate, and clarity about how the interview will be carried out. You can then mentally rehearse being in the interview, and practice being asked questions similar to those you answered on your application form, but perhaps more targeted at the job.

8. Control

Something that often causes people to feel stressed with interviews is that they worry about whether they will get the job or not, and they worry about what the interviewers will think of them. None of this is under your control as the interviewee, so if you decide to worry about it, that worry isn't going to make them offer you the job, or make the interviewers like you. Conversely, it might increase anxiety levels, which could reduce your ability to think as well as you can normally, and so you may give answers which aren't as good as they could be. You want to focus on what is within your control, and judge yourself only by that. In this way, you can give the answers to the best of your ability; you can arrive in good time for the interview, you smile and make eye contact, etc., and you can be kind and polite. If you have done your best and you don't get offered the job, then you can ask for feedback and learn from it, practicing what you need to, for next time. All it means is that someone else was felt to be more appropriate for the role according to the interviewers. If 50 or 100 people applied for the job, and you got an interview against the top ten applicants, that is an achievement, even if you aren't the final chosen one. If you never seem to get offered interviews, then you need to work with someone on writing out applications to make sure you are answering the questions correctly and in the way the companies are likely to want. Sometimes, you can contact the companies you have applied for and ask them if they can give you feedback about why you weren't selected. If there is a pattern to this, you can learn what you need to change. It could be that you apply for jobs which require a higher skill level so you never get picked, or that you make the same mistake on each application, in the way you fill it in.

9. Answers

When you are answering interviewers' questions, you want to draw on examples from things you have done. The examples don't necessarily have to be things you have done in other jobs, it could be from hobbies, or interests, or just everyday life. You want to think about your answers, because when you answer you want to be brief - not single-word brief, but perhaps a minute or two to give each answer, or each point if the answer requires more than one point to it based on the question. You don't want to just talk on and on.

10. Voice

How you use your voice is important. You want to talk with melody to your voice. You don't want to just talk at the interviewers in a slow, monotonous drawl. You also want to talk at a comfortable pace. So, if you normally talk very slowly, you may want to pick up the speed of your voice a little. You don't want to go too far from your normal voice, but you want to have some character to it. You can practice at home in a mirror, or recording your voice and listening back to it. Most people don't like the sound of their own voice, so you will have to get used to it, but once you are, you can notice whether you talk monotonously, or slowly, and what you need to change, and practice these changes.

Dan Jones

CHAPTER SEVEN

Being A Friend, Colleague, Or In A Relationship With Someone With Asperger's

1. Patience

Something a friend, colleague or partner of someone with Asperger's needs is patience. There will be times they struggle and get anxious, or frustrated, or emotional, or suddenly have black-and-white thinking. They may get the wrong end of the stick, or say something which upsets you, despite not intending to do so, or they can't do things you think are easy, and they need your help to do those things.

2. Expectations

The person with Asperger's may not think about you often when you are not physically present, or perhaps on their computer screen on a social network, so they may rarely instigate communication. This doesn't mean they don't care, just that they think differently about things, including what caring means to them. For example, for me, if I choose to have someone in my life at all, and communicate or interact with them, then I care. You may need to help them to do things you find easy; perhaps you can't understand why they find it so difficult, or why they get so stressed by certain things. They may not say 'hello' or 'good morning' or 'goodbye', or ask how you are doing, or if you have had a good day. Again, this doesn't mean they don't care. As you get to know them, you will learn what your expectations should be.

3. Space

The person with Asperger's is likely to want space - both their own physical space, and space from you and other people. They may keep themselves to themselves at times. This doesn't mean they are arrogant, or rude, just that they need their own space.

4. Direct yet friendly

The person with Asperger's is likely to be direct and honest with you, and they are likely to prefer the same back, even if they get told something upsetting. At least, that way, it isn't ambiguous where they get anxious trying to work out what you mean. You should be direct, yet friendly - not direct in an attacking or judgemental-sounding way. The aim is to minimise uncertainty and ambiguity, not to be horrible to someone.

5. Calm

The person with Asperger's will most likely find certain situations cause anxiety, especially high-sensory situations and those with high levels of uncertainty. Communicating calmly with them will help them to calm down. Just like most people, telling them to be calm is unlikely to work; it may make them angrier or more anxious.

6. Accepting of their differences

The person with Asperger's will have differences in how they think about things, and in what they do. They may do behaviours which seem odd, or have opinions and views which you find frustrating to hear or argue against, but they are who they are. Everyone is different, that is the one similarity we all share. Judging their differences or making fun of them, doesn't help. What is needed is acceptance - knowledge that it is okay for them to be themselves, that they don't have to change to fit a way they *should* be.

7. Supportive

The person with Asperger's will need those around them to be supportive. If they can't do something, then help them to do it, encourage them with it, help them to learn the necessary skills. For example, I still struggle to talk on the telephone. If I have to make a call to someone I don't know, it can take me weeks or months before I'm able to make that call.

Encouragement and support, and belief in me, helps me do things like that much quicker.

8. Taking the lead

The Asperger's person may worry about accidentally doing something wrong which could cause offense or upset. For example, I know with myself and dating, I worry about intimacy, even if I think I would like to do something, I worry I may be misreading the signs and that my behaviour of going in for a kiss or whatever may be seen as attempted sexual assault. So sometimes I won't try at all; rather, I will hope the other person likes me enough to take the lead, which lets me know what they are comfortable with. This goes for other social situations as well. I would never kiss or hug someone to greet them or to say goodbye because I wouldn't want my actions to be misunderstood, but I will (reluctantly) accept others kissing or hugging me to greet me or say goodbye. There are many situations which crop up where the person with Asperger's struggles to work out what is socially acceptable in that situation. This could be from telling jokes to particular behaviours; it is helpful when friends, family, loved ones and work colleagues take the lead. Unfortunately, those with Asperger's may follow the lead of someone who is encouraging them to do things which aren't appropriate behaviours, and because of the context, they don't realise they are being made to do things they shouldn't be doing.

CHAPTER EIGHT

Being An Employer Of Someone With Asperger's

1. Supportive

An employee with Asperger's will need to have a supportive and patient manager. They may take longer to do certain tasks, and may really struggle to do some things at all, yet other things they will have no problem doing. So, they may struggle to make the phone calls you have asked them to make, but they will have their records up-to-date, and spreadsheets done, and data collected and collated ready for presentation. Just because they don't do something, or because they take a long time to do something, this should result in conversations about how to overcome the issue, which could be learning certain skills, mentoring, etc. All of this should be looked at before taking disciplinary action or dismissal.

2. Accepting of their differences

The employee with Asperger's will think about things differently. You should utilise this. In meetings where everyone gives similar answers to questions, the person with Asperger's is likely to have a different perspective because they will see things as patterns differently to other colleagues. They are also likely to focus on simplicity, for example, noticing a simple solution others may miss. When I worked in children's homes, I solved a bullying problem caused due to a child not bathing, by taking the child swimming multiple times per week; when I worked in mental health, a resident was being bullied due to his OCD which led to him urinating everywhere and not being willing to touch dirt, so all mess he made stayed where it was. I gave him a box of sterile latex gloves, and he was immediately able to clean up after himself, so the bullying stopped.

The employee with Asperger's may seem unusual, or may come across as single-minded because they either don't engage in conversations, or if they do, it is all about what they are interested in. Or there may be long silences when with them, or unusual behaviours or mannerisms, or eye contact. It is important to accept these differences, and seeing how their uniqueness can be helpful within their role in the workplace.

3. Utilise their skills and interests

The employee with Asperger's will have many skills, as well as becoming very focused on interests. Every job I've done I've become obsessed with, because I want to know everything there is to know about things when I do them. So, when I started working in parenting support, I wanted to know everything about parenting research and data, and about our parenting work effectiveness, and different parenting programmes and their effectiveness. So, it made sense to utilise my obsessiveness and interest because I knew more about the subject than most other people due to being so obsessed. People feel valued when their skills are used and acknowledged; this could be problem-solving skills, creativity, an interest, or anything else. It is important to look at the employee from a strengths perspective, rather than a deficit perspective.

4. Clear communication and expectations

You should have clear communication with and expectations of the employee with Asperger's. Make sure you explain things to them clearly, and ask them to let you know what they will be doing, so that you know they have understood. It is helpful to talk with them to learn about them, so that you can better understand and support them. You also want to make sure they are understanding everything you are asking of them. They will be unlikely to come to talk to you. So, if you have given them work to do and you want to be told once they have completed it, if you haven't specifically told them to do so, they are likely to just move on to the next task once that one is complete.

You can't expect them to react to things like other employees. They may have odd responses to questions because they take things literally. They may be blunt and truthful about something with you, or with other staff, and not realise they have hurt someone's feelings, or they may struggle to do certain roles. They may even, in extreme cases, walk out of work because something was changed. The employee with Asperger's will most likely like structure and routine, and so if they have their desk moved or other people use their desk, this could cause anxiety, or even make them quit. If they are asked to do a job or role they don't normally do, they may just walk out rather than do that job.

5. Work environment

The employee's work environment is very important. They are unlikely to be able to work well in noisy environments, or where there is lots of sensory input. This could be strip lighting (which flashes, although not everyone notices this), or motion-sensor lighting which is constantly turning on and off, or people constantly walking past their field of view, or talking across them. It is best to work with the employee, perhaps with occupational health support, to look at what environment is best suited to them, and whether they need any equipment to be able to do their job effectively. It could be that they would benefit from headphones to cut out the noise if they were going to be working in an office.

Asperger's Syndrome: Tips & Strategies

Printed in Great Britain
by Amazon